Welcome to
BASIC Grammar

3

KUMSUNG

About This Book

개념 학습

✚ 초등학생이 꼭 알아야 할 문법 개념을 쉽게 설명해요.

친구들의 문법 도우미! 니콜 선생님의 쉽고 재미있는 설명을 들으면 문법 개념이 머리에 쏙쏙! 문법 실력은 쑥쑥!

PC www.englishbuddy.kr에서도 볼 수 있어요.

문제 풀이

✚ Quick Check-Up ➡ 다양한 유형의 exercise ➡ Fun Wrap-Up 순으로 문제를 제시하여 체계적으로 학습할 수 있어요.

Step 1

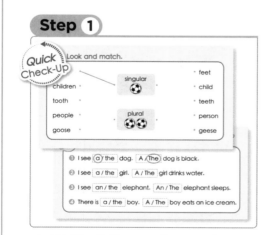

간단한 문제를 풀어보며 문법 개념을 잘 이해했는지 확인해요.

Step 2

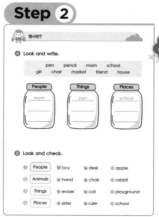

다양한 유형의 문제를 풀어보며 실력을 다져요.

Step 3

미로 찾기, 색칠하기 등 재미있는 활동으로 학습한 내용을 복습하며 마무리해요.

Contents 3

Chapter 9 의문사와 접속사

Lesson 41	의문사	• 의문사의 종류 • 의문사 있는 의문문	6
Lesson 42	의문대명사, 의문형용사	• 의문대명사 • 의문형용사	12
Lesson 43	의문부사	• when, where, why, how • how many, how much	18
Lesson 44	접속사 1	• and, but • or	24
Lesson 45	접속사 2	• before, after • so, because	30
Lesson 46	기수, 서수	• 기수와 서수의 의미 • 연도, 날짜, 화폐, 전화번호 읽기	36
Basic Test			42

Chapter 10 문장의 종류

Lesson 47	명령문, 제안문	• 명령문 • 제안문	46
Lesson 48	감탄문	• How 감탄문 • What 감탄문	52
Lesson 49	비인칭 주어 it	• 비인칭 주어 it (1) • 비인칭 주어 it (2)	58
Basic Test			64

Chapter 11 과거 시제

Lesson 50	Be동사: 과거형	• 주어의 인칭에 따른 변화 • 주어의 수에 따른 변화	68
Lesson 51	Be동사 과거 시제: 부정문	• was not, were not • wasn't, weren't	74
Lesson 52	Be동사 과거 시제: 의문문	• 질문하기 • 대답하기	80
Lesson 53	일반동사: 과거 시제 1	• 규칙 변화 (1) • 규칙 변화 (2)	86
Lesson 54	일반동사: 과거 시제 2	• 불규칙 변화 (1) • 불규칙 변화 (2)	92
Lesson 55	일반동사 과거 시제: 부정문	• did not • didn't	98
Lesson 56	일반동사 과거 시제: 의문문	• Did∼? • 의문사+did∼?	104
Lesson 57	과거 진행형	• 긍정문 • 부정문	110
Lesson 58	과거 진행형: 의문문	• yes/no 의문문 • 의문사 있는 의문문	116
Basic Test			122

Chapter 12 미래 시제

Lesson 59	미래 시제	• will • be going to	126
Lesson 60	미래 시제: 의문문	• will 의문문 • be going to 의문문	132
Basic Test			138
Answers			141
Activity Cards & Paper Cube			167
Appendix			171

Chapter 9

의문사와
접속사

Lesson 41   의문사

Lesson 42   의문대명사, 의문형용사

Lesson 43   의문부사

Lesson 44   접속사 1

Lesson 45   접속사 2

Lesson 46   기수, 서수

I can do it!

의문사의 종류

❀ '누가, 무엇을, 언제, 어디서, 어떻게, 왜?'와 같은 말을 의문사라고 해요.
의문사의 종류와 쓰임새는 다음과 같아요.

who	누구	**Who** is he?
what	무엇	**What** is your phone number?
when	언제	**When** is your birthday?
where	어디서	**Where** are you from?
why	왜	**Why** are you crying?
how	어떻게	**How** are you?

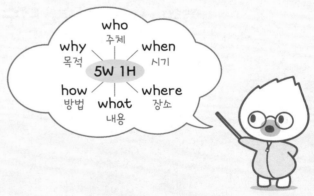

Quick Check-Up

Check the *question words*.

• question word 의문사

☐ who   ☐ how   ☐ why

☐ because   ☐ then   ☐ however

☐ they   ☐ where   ☑ when

☐ there   ☐ so   ☐ what

의문사의 종류

A Circle the correct *question words.*

① ⟨When⟩ / Where | is your birthday?

② How / Who | can you make it?

③ What / When | do you like?

④ Why / Who | is your best friend?

⑤ How / What | are you today?

B Complete the each dialogue.

What   When   Where   How   Why

① ___What___ is his name?   - It's John.

② _____ is her birthday?   - It's on June 3.

③ _____ does John live?   - He lives in Seoul.

④ _____ is your teacher?   - He is good.

⑤ _____ are you late?   - I missed the train.

 **Fill in the blanks.**

_____ Where _____ is my watch?
- It's on the table.

_____ is that man?
- It's Tom's dad.

_____ is he doing?
- He is working.

_____ does he come?
- This afternoon.

_____ are you?
- I'm good.

_____ are you happy?
- Because I found my cat.

의문사

의문사 있는 의문문

❀ 의문사를 사용한 의문문은 다음과 같이 나타내요.

be동사인 경우	[의문사+be동사+주어 ~?] **Who are** you?　　**Who is** he? **Where is** my gift?　　**Where are** my socks? **Why is** she so happy?　　**When is** your birthday?
일반동사인 경우	[의문사+do(does)+주어+동사원형 ~?] **What do** you **have**?　　**What does** she **read**? **Why do** you **study** hard?　　**Why does** he **run**? **Where do** you **go**?　　**Where does** she **go**?

Quick Check-Up — Circle the correct ones.

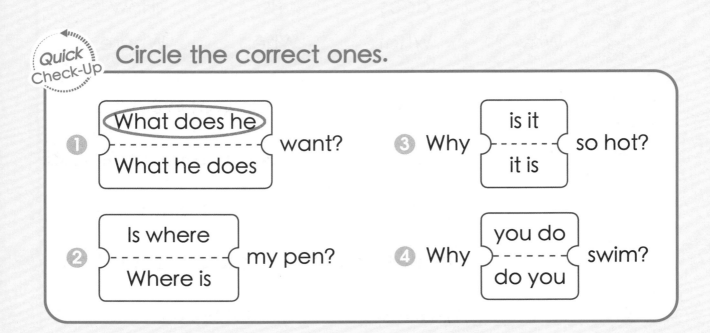

❶ (What does he) / What he does 〉 want?

❷ Is where / Where is 〉 my pen?

❸ Why 〈 is it / it is 〉 so hot?

❹ Why 〈 you do / do you 〉 swim?

A Unscramble the sentences.

1 do / Why / study math? / you

   Why do you study math?

2 you / do / When / go to bed?

   _____

3 feel? / you / How / do

   _____

B Use the words to complete the questions.

do	does	is	How
Why	What	When	Where

1 Where does she live? — She lives in Busan.

2 _____ _____ you cry? — Because the movie is sad.

3 _____ _____ your birthday? — It is on March 5.

4 _____ _____ he need a fan? — Because it's very hot.

5 _____ _____ you feel? — I feel great.

 **Fun Wrap-Up!** Look and answer.

1. **Where is Sam?**   - <u>He is in front of the bushes.</u>

2. **Who drinks juice?**   - _____

3. **What does Suzy eat?**   - _____

42

의문대명사, 의문형용사

의문대명사

❉ 의문대명사는 대명사의 역할을 하기 때문에, 뒤에 주어나 목적어가 필요 없어요.

사람	who	**Who** can solve this problem**?** **Who** told you**?**
사물	what	**What** do you want**?** **What** happened**?**
사람, 사물	which	**Which** is longer, this snake or that snake**?**

which는 A 또는 B 중 선택을 물을 때 사용해요.

 Circle the correct ones.

❶ ⟨Who⟩/ When opens the box?

❷ How / Which is shorter?

❸ Who / Where starts first?

❹ Which / How comes first?

❺ What / Where does she want?

의문대명사

A Read and mark ○ or ✗.

1 Who makes a noise? ⸻ ○

2 Who do you want to eat, pizza or salad? ⸻ ☐

3 What makes you cry? ⸻ ☐

4 Which is yours? ⸻ ☐

5 How likes apples? ⸻ ☐

B Read and match.

1 _____ do you like better, this or that?

2 _____ can read this book?

3 _____ makes him so sad?

4 _____ can solve the problem?

5 _____ do you want?

Who

What

Which

Fun Wrap-Up! Write the correct *question words*.

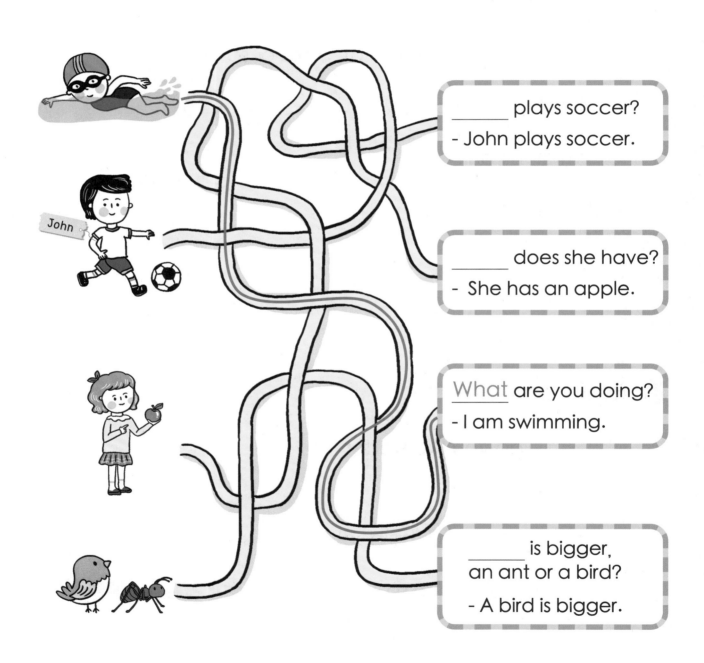

_____ plays soccer?
- John plays soccer.

_____ does she have?
- She has an apple.

<u>What</u> are you doing?
- I am swimming.

_____ is bigger,
an ant or a bird?
- A bird is bigger.

의문대명사, 의문형용사

의문형용사

🔅 의문형용사는 의문을 나타내는 형용사예요. 형태는 [의문형용사＋명사]예요.

What book do you read?　　　**Whose** hat is this?

사물	what＋명사	**What color** do you like**?** **What time** do you go to bed**?**
사람	whose＋명사	**Whose bag** is this**?** **Whose pen** is that**?**
선택	which＋명사	**Which animal** do you like, a puppy or a cat**?**

Quick Check-Up　Circle the correct ones.

① How /(What) color is it?

② What / Where time do you go to school?

③ Whose / Who car is this?

④ Who / Whose notebook is that?

⑤ Whose / Which color do you want, red or blue?

의문형용사

A Unscramble the sentences.

1 works / Whose / mother / at school?

Whose mother works at school?

2 Which / dress / I / should / wear?

_____

3 necklace / is / Whose / this?

_____

B Fill in the blanks with the given words.

What	Which	Whose

1 _____ computer is this?

2 _____Whose_____ song are you singing?

3 _____ time do you get up?

4 _____ kinds of books do you need?

 **Read and color.**

What    Whose ████   Which ████

size is this coat?

cup is yours?

umbrella is this?

time do you go to school?

color do you like?

의문부사

when, where, why, how

❀ 의문부사를 사용한 의문문은 [의문사＋do(es)＋주어＋동사원형 ～?], [의문사＋be동사＋주어 ～?] 형태로 나타내요. 의문부사의 종류와 쓰임새는 아래와 같아요.

when	언제	**When** do you go home**?**
where	어디서	**Where** do you read books**?**
why	왜	**Why** do you exercise**?**
how	어떻게	**How** do you go to school**?**
	얼마나	**How** old is this desk**?**

❀ 나이는 How old ～?
❀ 길이, 소요 시간은 How long ～?
❀ 빈도는 How often ～?
❀ 깊이는 How deep ～?으로 물어볼 수 있어요.

 Circle the correct ones.

❶ ⟨When⟩ / Where is your birthday?

❷ What / Where do you go?

❸ Why / How does she look so happy?

❹ Where / How do you feel?

❺ How / Why long is the bridge?

when, where, why, how

A Correct and rewrite the sentences.

1 ~~When~~ often do you visit your grandma?

How often do you visit your grandma?

2 **What** do you go to school?

_____

3 **Why** deep is the river?

_____

B Choose the best word to finish the *asking sentence*.

How	When	Where	Why

1 _____How_____ do you know him?

2 _____ is my wallet?

3 _____ are you crying?

4 _____ fast is this train?

5 _____ does the movie start?

when, where, why, how

 Follow, write, and match.

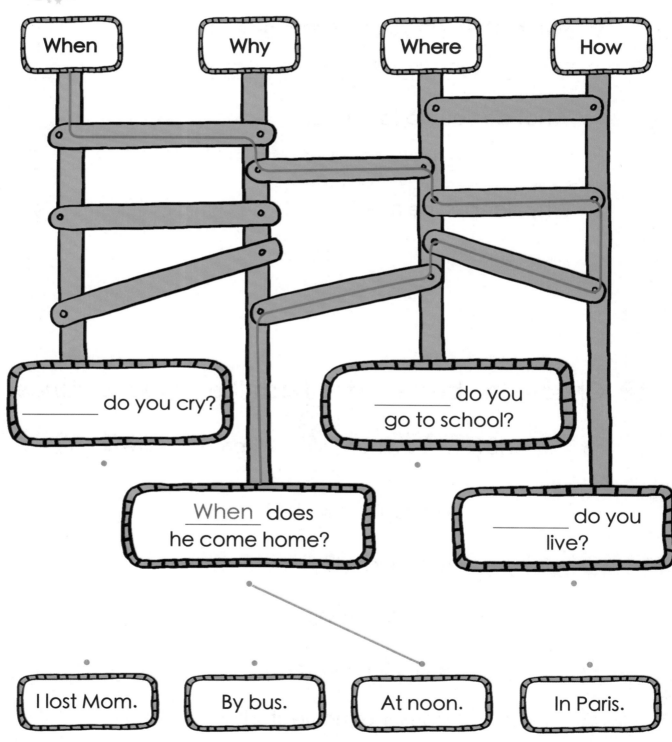

When | Why | Where | How

_____ do you cry?

_____ do you go to school?

<u>When</u> does he come home?

_____ do you live?

I lost Mom. | By bus. | At noon. | In Paris.

how many, how much

✿ 어떤 것의 수나 양을 물을 때에는 [how many/much+명사 ～?] 형태로 표현해요. how many나 how much의 쓰임새는 명사의 종류에 따라 달라요.

how many	셀 수 **있는** 명사 복수형	(수가) 얼마나 많은
how much	셀 수 **없는** 명사	(양이) 얼마나 많은, (값이) 얼마

How many books
does she have?

How much bread
do you eat?

Circle the correct ones.

① How many /(How much) water do you drink?

② How many / How much snowmen do you make?

③ How many / How much pens does the boy have?

④ How many / How much is this ring?

⑤ How many / How much words does she know?

how many, how much

A Read and mark ○ or ✕.

1. How many students do you teach? .... ○

2. How many money do you need? ....

3. How many times did you read the book? ....

4. How many milk does he need? ....

B Choose and write.

many	much

1. How __much__ is the car?

2. How _____ water do you use a day?

3. How _____ cups do we need?

4. How _____ pairs of shoes does she have?

5. How _____ days do I have to wait?

6. How _____ money do you need?

7. How _____ tables are there in the classroom?

Follow the correct ones.

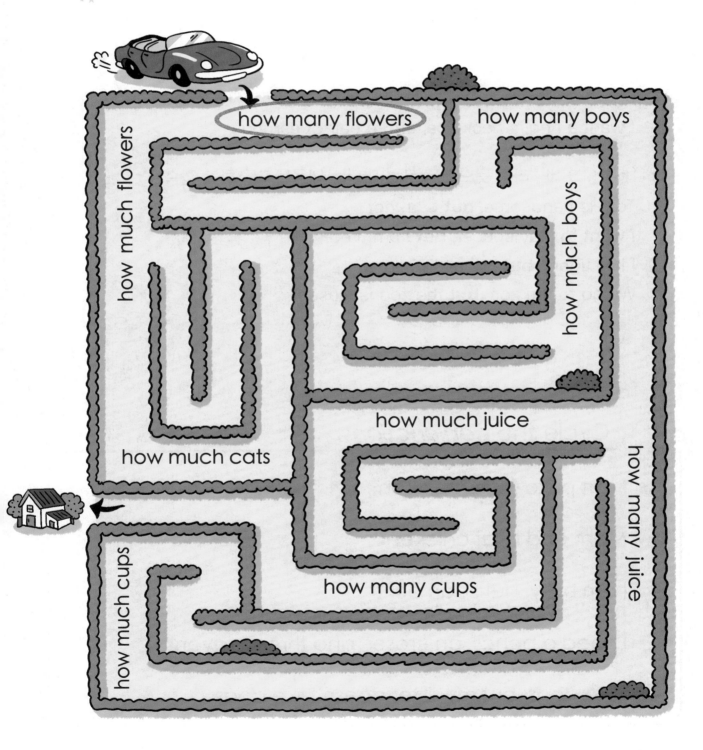

how many flowers

how many boys

how much flowers

how much boys

how much cats

how much juice

how much cups

how many cups

how many juice

접속사 1

and, but

❋ **and**: '그리고'라는 뜻으로 서로 비슷한 내용을 연결하는 접속사

Tom **and** John go to school.   The pigs sit **and** play.

She is pretty **and** smart.   He comes **and** sits.

3개 이상의 단어를 나열할 때는 제일 마지막 단어 앞에만 **and**를 써 줘요.

I want a ring, a necklace, **and** a pair of earrings.

❋ **but**: '그러나'라는 뜻으로 서로 반대되는 내용을 연결하는 접속사

Tom is handsome, **but** I am not.

I want to play soccer, **but** I am tired.

I like tigers, **but** I don't like lions.

We go to the zoo, **but** the zoo is closed.

단어와 단어, 구와 구,
문장과 문장을 연결해 주는 것을
접속사라고 해요.

Quick Check-Up — Circle the *conjunctions*.

• conjunction 접속사

❶ I eat pizza (and) chicken.

❷ Mom and I eat chicken.

❸ I am busy, but I can do it.

❹ I need a pencil, an eraser, and three crayons.

❺ I like dogs, but my sister doesn't like dogs.

and, but

A **Read and choose.**

1 Mike ⟨and⟩/ but I need a lot of money.

2 He is handsome and / but kind.

3 She likes pizza, and / but she doesn't like salad.

4 It's Saturday, and / but I don't have any plans.

5 My birthday is today, and / but I have a party.

B **Read and mark ○ or ✕.**

1 My cat is cute and sweet. ⸺ ○

2 It's cold today, but I don't have a jacket. ⸺ ☐

3 I play the piano, and I don't play the guitar. ⸺ ☐

4 She likes English, and he doesn't like English. ⸺ ☐

5 I cut my finger, but I don't cry. ⸺ ☐

 **and, but**

 **Complete the sentence and draw it.**

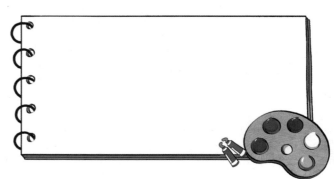

① I like pizza, and my brother _____ too.

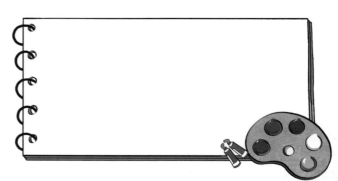

② I play soccer, but I don't play _____ .

③ I have a puppy, but you _____ .

44

접속사 1

or

✿ or: '또는'이라는 뜻으로 어떤 것들 중 하나를 선택할 때 사용하는 접속사

Which do you like better, pizza **or** pasta?

Which do you want to buy, this pencil **or** that pencil?

Which do you want to play, soccer **or** tennis?

Do you have any sisters **or** brothers?

You can go to the zoo by bus **or** by subway.

Are you coming **or** not?

It can be black **or** grey.

Quick Check-Up Circle the correct ones.

① I know the answer, (but) / or I can't tell you.

② Is it a boy and / or a girl?

③ You can go to the zoo by bus but / or by taxi.

④ Who opens the door, Jane but / or Tom?

or

A Correct and rewrite.

1. I want to be a doctor ~~but~~ a nurse in the future.

   I want to be a doctor or a nurse in the future.

2. Do you have any sisters **but** brothers?

   _____

3. Is your brother older **and** younger than you?

   _____

B Fill in the blanks.

and	but	or

1. Do we take a train __or__ a bus?

2. Jim can't speak Japanese, _____ he can speak English.

3. Which do you like better, apples _____ bananas?

4. Mary goes shopping, _____ she buys a dress.

Fun Wrap-Up! **Read and write.**

and	but	or

❶ Dad, Mom, my sister, ___and___ I go to the zoo.

❷ We can go there by bus _____ by subway.

❸ We pack sandwiches _____ some fruits for lunch.

❹ At the zoo, we see lions _____ tigers.

❺ I am scared, _____ I go closer to the cage.

접속사 2

before, after

❀ before: ～하기 전에

I wash my hands **before** I have a meal.

He goes home **before** it gets dark.

I wash my face **before** I go to school.

❀ after: ～한 후에

She brushes her teeth **after** she has a meal.

I put the toys away **after** I play with them.

I put on my shoes **after** I put on my socks.

Quick
Check-Up ── Circle the correct ones.

❶ Sam watches TV ⟩ **before** / after ⟨ he plays soccer.

❷ Sam plays soccer ⟩ before / after ⟨ he watches TV.

before, after

A Fill in the blanks.

| before | after |

1. I raise my hand __before__ I ask a question.

2. I wash my face __b_____ I go to school.

3. I must go home __b_____ it gets dark.

4. I go to bed __a_____ I take a shower.

5. I have breakfast __a_____ I get up.

B Read and match.

1. I put on my socks _____
   I put on my shoes.

2. I wash the dishes _____
   I have a meal.

3. I brush my teeth _____
   I have a meal.

before

after

before, after

Fun Wrap-Up! Cut and paste.

1 I wash fruits before I eat them.

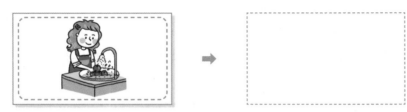

2 I dry my hair after I wash my hair.

3 I make my bed after I get up in the morning.

※ 아래와 동일한 카드가 167쪽에 있습니다. 해당 페이지의 카드를 사용하세요.

Go to p. 167

so, because

❀ so : 그래서

We play in the room **so** the room is messy.

I am tired **so** I don't play tennis.

The baby falls down **so** he cries.

It is rainy **so** I need an umbrella.

❀ because : 왜냐하면

The girl is happy **because** she has an ice cream.

I am sad **because** I lost my puppy.

I can't sleep **because** it's too noisy.

so는 결과, because는 원인을
나타내는 접속사예요.

Quick Check-Up Circle the correct ones.

① I am tired ⟨ **so** / because ⟩ I go to bed earlier.

② We like to play with toys ⟨ so / **because** ⟩ it is fun.

③ I wash my toys ⟨ so / **because** ⟩ they are dirty.

so, because

A Read and mark O or X.

1. He forgets his bag so he can't do his homework. ⟶ O

2. It's cold outside because I wear a coat. ⟶ ☐

3. I buy a gift so it's her birthday. ⟶ ☐

4. I should stay in bed so I am sick. ⟶ ☐

5. I hurt my leg because I cry. ⟶ ☐

B Read and write.

because	so

1. The man is hungry _____so_____ he gets a snack.

2. I study hard _____ I have a test.

3. He needs a fan _____ it is summer.

4. I get up late _____ I miss the school bus.

5. Jane is sick _____ she can't go to school.

so   because

| I hurt my leg | It's cold | They can't play outside | I am sad |

_____
I wear a coat.

_____
I lost my cat.

___so___ I can't play soccer.

_____
it's raining.

Lesson

46

기수, 서수

기수와 서수의 의미

✿ 수에는 하나, 둘, 셋처럼 개수를 나타내는 '기수'와, 첫 번째, 두 번째, 세 번째 처럼 순서를 나타내는 '서수'가 있어요. 서수 앞에는 반드시 **the**를 붙여 줘요.

- 기수: one, two, three...　　　There are **two** apples.
- 서수: first, second, third...　　Monday is **the first** day of the week.

	기수	서수		기수	서수		기수	서수
1	one	first	11	eleven	eleven**th**	30	thirty	thirtie**th**
2	two	second	12	twelve	twel**fth**	40	forty	fortie**th**
3	three	third	13	thirteen	thirteen**th**	50	fifty	fiftie**th**
4	four	four**th**	14	fourteen	fourteen**th**	60	sixty	sixtie**th**
5	five	fif**th**	15	fifteen	fifteen**th**	70	seventy	seventie**th**
6	six	six**th**	16	sixteen	sixteen**th**	80	eighty	eightie**th**
7	seven	seven**th**	17	seventeen	seventeen**th**	90	ninety	ninetie**th**
8	eight	eigh**th**	18	eighteen	eighteen**th**	100	one hundred	one hundred**th**
9	nine	nin**th**	19	nineteen	nineteen**th**			
10	ten	ten**th**	20	twenty	twentie**th**			

Quick Check-Up — ## Check the correct ones.

- ☑ one – first
- ☐ three – third
- ☐ five – fiveth
- ☐ eleven – eleventh
- ☐ twenty – twentyth
- ☐ sixty – sixtieth

기수와 서수의 의미

A Write the *ordinal numbers* in order.

| fourth | seventh | second | ninth |

first → *second* → third → _____ → fifth

→ sixth → _____ → eighth → _____ → tenth

B Read and match.

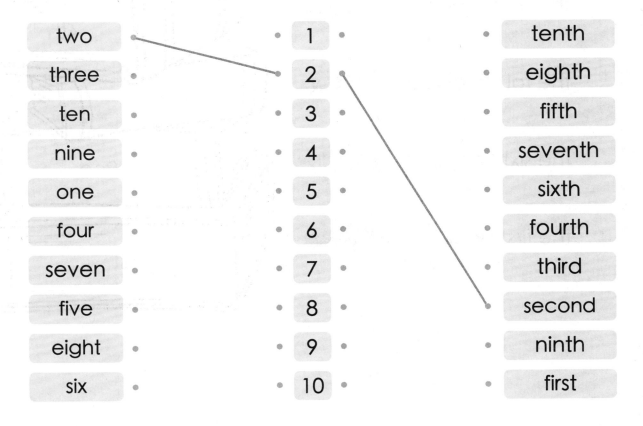

two		1		tenth
three		2		eighth
ten		3		fifth
nine		4		seventh
one		5		sixth
four		6		fourth
seven		7		third
five		8		second
eight		9		ninth
six		10		first

Read and color.

the seventh book

the second book

the fifth book

the third book

the fourth book

the sixth book

the first book

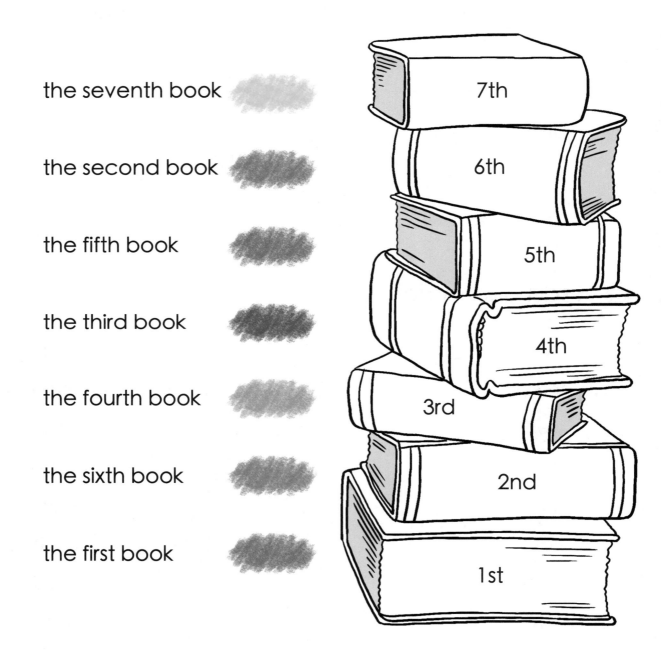

연도, 날짜, 화폐, 전화번호 읽기

❀ 연도 읽기

• 두 자리씩 끊어 읽어요.

1978년 → nineteen seventy eight   1890년 → eighteen ninety

• 2000년도 이후부터는 일반 숫자처럼 읽어도 돼요.

2002년 → two thousand and two

❀ 날짜 읽기: 요일-월-일-연도 순으로 표현해요. 날짜는 서수로 읽어요.

Monday, May 11, 2018

❀ 돈 읽기: 화폐 단위와 함께 표현해요.

$50 → fifty dollars $35 → thirty five dollars

❀ 전화번호: 한 자리씩 기수로 읽어요. 숫자 0은 **oh** 또는 **zero**로 읽어요.

123-9087 → one two three, nine oh eight seven

May 11은 May 11th로도 쓰고,
May eleventh로 읽어요.

Quick
Check-Up

Check the correct ones.

☑ 1978년 – nineteen seventy eight   ☐ January thirteen

☐ $100 – one hundred dollars   ☐ May eleventh

A Read and mark ○ or ✗.

1 1985년 ➡ nineteen eighty fifth ⋯⋯⋯⋯⋯⋯⋯⋯⋯⋯⋯⋯⋯⋯ ✗

2 $25 ➡ twenty five dollars ⋯⋯⋯⋯⋯⋯⋯⋯⋯⋯⋯⋯⋯⋯⋯ ☐

3 011-232-9990

➡ zero one one, two three two, nine nine nine oh ⋯ ☐

4 May 14 ➡ May fourteenth ⋯⋯⋯⋯⋯⋯⋯⋯⋯⋯⋯⋯⋯⋯⋯⋯ ☐

B Look and write.

1 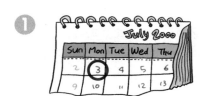 July 3

July third

2  $20

_____

3

_____

Tuesday, June 14, 2018

Today was the wonderful day.

On my way to school, I met an old lady.

She carried a heavy bag, so I helped her.

She asked me my phone number.

I gave her Mom's number, 010-123-4567.

When I arrived home, Mom said, "I heard you helped an

old lady. I'm proud of you." Mom gave me $10.

I felt great. What a good day!

A Choose the correct answers.

1 _____ is your birthday?

   ① What   ② Where   ③ When

2 _____ color do you want, red or blue?

   ① Which   ② Whose   ③ Who

3 _____ often do you visit your grandma?

   ① When   ② How   ③ Where

4 She likes pizza, _____ she doesn't like salad.

   ① and   ② or   ③ but

5 I wash my face _____ I go to school.

   ① before   ② after   ③ but

B Fill in the blanks.

July third	so	or	What

1 It can be black _____ grey.

2 Tomorrow is _____.

3 _____ time do you go to bed?

4 The baby falls down _____ he cries.

C Unscramble the sentences.

1 it? / can / you / make / How

_____

2 at school? / mother / Whose / works

_____

3 times / the book? / did / read / How many / you

_____

4 too / can't / sleep / I / because / it's / noisy.

_____

D Answer the questions.

1 What's the date today?

_____

2 How are you today?

_____

3 Which do you like better, apples or oranges?

_____

4 What do you do before you go to bed?

_____

Lesson 47   명령문, 제안문

Lesson 48   감탄문

Lesson 49   비인칭 주어 it

I can do it!

명령문

✿ '~해라'라는 뜻의 명령문은 주어 없이 동사원형으로 시작해요.

You study hard. → **Study** hard.

You give me a pen. → **Give** me a pen.

✿ 부정 명령문은 '~하지 마'라는 뜻으로 [Do not/Don't+동사원형 ~.]
으로 나타내요.

You don't play soccer. → **Don't play** soccer.

You don't tell a lie. → **Don't tell** a lie.

✿ 동사가 be동사(am, are, is)일 경우에는 원형인 be를 써요.

You **are** nice to your friends. → **Be** nice to your friends.

You **are** quiet. → **Be** quiet.

Quick Check-Up — Check the correct ones.

☑ Pick up the book.   ☐ Doesn't swim in the lake.

☐ Goes to the store.   ☐ Give me the pen.

☐ Does not run.   ☐ Does pass me the book.

☐ Be honest.   ☐ You quiet.

☐ Do it now.   ☐ Don't tell a lie.

명령문

A **Correct and rewrite.**

① ~~Takes~~ me to the store.   Take me to the store.

② **Writing** your name on the paper.

_____

③ **Not** leave your bike in the park.

_____

④ **Are** careful.   _____

⑤ **Does** not take the bus.   _____

B **Read and circle.**

① (Wipe) / Wipes   the floor.

② Don't / Doesn't   give up.

③ Give / Giving   me some water.

④ Not / Don't   be late.

⑤ Wait / Waiting   for me.

 Fill in the blanks.

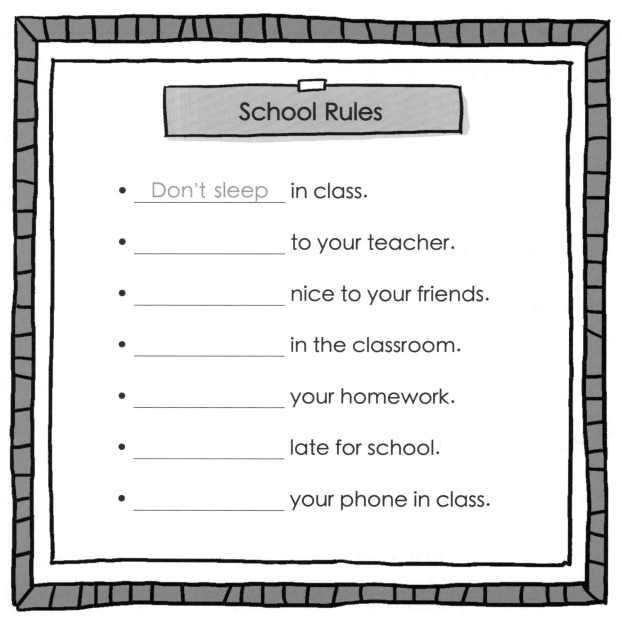

School Rules

- _Don't sleep_ in class.

- _____ to your teacher.

- _____ nice to your friends.

- _____ in the classroom.

- _____ your homework.

- _____ late for school.

- _____ your phone in class.

Don't use	Be	Don't be	Do
Don't run	Listen	Don't sleep	

제안문

❀ [Let's+동사원형]을 사용해서 '우리 ~하자'라고 제안을 할 수 있어요.

Let's go shopping.   **Let's be** quiet.

❀ '우리 ~하지 말자'라고 표현할 때에는 [Let's not+동사원형] 형태를 사용해요.

Let's not go shopping.   **Let's not be** quiet.

❀ 제안에 대한 대답은 다음과 같이 해요.
- 긍정: Good. / Great. / Sure.
- 부정: Sorry, I can't. / I'm sorry, but I can't.

Quick Check-Up — Circle the correct ones.

① Let's 〔dance〕/ dancing .

② Let's │ leave / be leaving │ him alone.

③ Let's │ not wait / wait not │ for him.

④ Let's │ play / plays │ soccer.

⑤ Let's │ not tell / tell not │ it to Mom.

⑥ Let's │ do / does │ our best.

A Read and mark ○ or ✕.

1. Let's goes on a picnic. ⟶ ✕

2. Let's not make a noise. ⟶ ☐

3. Let's is honest. ⟶ ☐

4. Let's play baseball. ⟶ ☐

B Unscramble the sentences.

1. play / Let's / outside.

   Let's play outside.

2. tomorrow. / go fishing / Let's

   _____

3. not / Let's / on the street. / throw trash

   _____

4. fight / Let's / not / again.

   _____

1

Let's not ___draw on the desks___ .

2

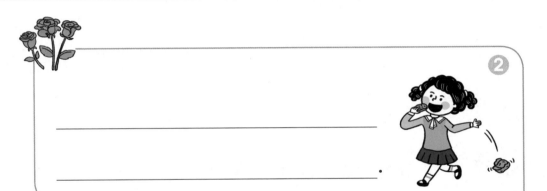

_____

_____ .

3

_____ .

• throw trash on the street

• be late

• draw on the desks

How 감탄문

❀ '와, 멋지다!', '깜짝이야!'처럼 감정을 나타내는 문장을 감탄문이라고 해요.
How로 시작하는 감탄문의 문장 순서는
[How+형용사/부사+(주어+동사)!]예요.

He is very smart.　　　→ **How smart** (he is)!

The baby is very cute.　→ **How cute** (the baby is)!

The party is fun.　　　→ **How fun** (the party is)!

감탄문에는 How로 시작하는 것과
What으로 시작하는 것이 있어요.

Quick Check-Up Circle the correct ones.

❶
How cute he is!
How he is cute!

❹
How is the nice dress!
How nice the dress is!

❷
How the tall girl is!
How tall the girl is!

❺
How large the park is!
How large the park is.

❸
How hot it is!
How hot is it!

❻
How fun the party is!
How is the party fun!

How 감탄문

A Unscramble the sentences.

1 How big / are! / his feet

How big his feet are!

2 your house / is! / How clean

_____

3 How delicious / the noodle / is!

_____

4 he / How fast / eats!

_____

B Correct and rewrite.

1 How fun ~~is the game~~!   How fun the game is!

2 How big her eyes are.   _____

3 How lazy **is she**!   _____

4 How **the river deep** is!   _____

5 How **you creative** are!   _____

How 감탄문

A country mouse visits his friend in a big city. The country mouse is surprised to see the city. The mouse says, "How big the city is!"

How tall the buildings are!
(tall / the buildings / are)

_____ !
(fast / the cars / go)

_____ !
(big / your house / is)

What 감탄문

❀ What으로 시작하는 감탄문은

[What＋a/an＋형용사＋명사＋(주어＋동사)!] 순서로 나타내요.

He is a great man. → **What a great man** (he is)!

It is a very old computer. → **What an old computer** (it is)!

It is a nice day. → **What a nice day** (it is)!

It is a very tall building. → **What a tall building** (it is)!

He is a handsome man. → **What a handsome man** (he is)!

Quick
Check-Up

Read and mark ○ or ✗.

1 What a big balloon is it! ⋯⋯⋯⋯⋯⋯⋯⋯⋯⋯⋯⋯⋯⋯ ✗

2 What a nice jacket! ⋯⋯⋯⋯⋯⋯⋯⋯⋯⋯⋯⋯⋯⋯⋯⋯⋯ ☐

3 What handsome man he is! ⋯⋯⋯⋯⋯⋯⋯⋯⋯⋯⋯⋯ ☐

4 What an old computer it is! ⋯⋯⋯⋯⋯⋯⋯⋯⋯⋯⋯ ☐

5 What nice day it is! ⋯⋯⋯⋯⋯⋯⋯⋯⋯⋯⋯⋯⋯⋯⋯⋯ ☐

6 What a funny story it is! ⋯⋯⋯⋯⋯⋯⋯⋯⋯⋯⋯⋯⋯ ☐

What 감탄문

A Unscramble the sentences.

1. this / is! / What / a / beautiful picture

   What a beautiful picture this is!

2. an / it / is! / interesting book / What

   _____

3. a / little hamster / What / is! / it

   _____

4. What / a / great idea / it / is!

   _____

B Change the sentences into their *exclamatory sentences*.

1. She is a great cook.

   What a great cook she is!

2. It is an amazing story.

   What _____

3. It is a cold day.

   What _____

Fun Wrap-Up!

Follow and write.

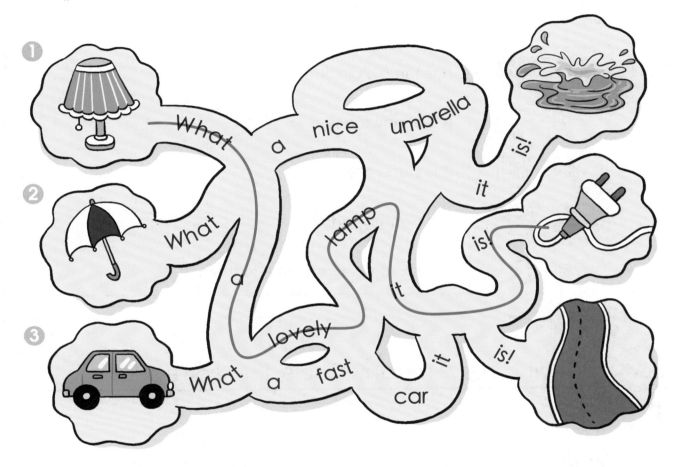

1   What a lovely lamp it is!

2   _____

3   _____

비인칭 주어 it

비인칭 주어 it (1)

✿ 비인칭 주어 it은 시간, 날씨, 날짜, 요일, 거리 등을 나타내요. 이때 it은 '그것'이라고 해석하지 않아요.

시간	⏰	**It** is three o'clock.
날씨	☁	**It** is windy today.
날짜	📅	**It** is December 25.
요일	📅	**It** is Sunday today.
거리	🚩	**It** is six meters from here to there.

Quick Check-Up — What does *It* mean? Circle the correct ones.

❶ It is ten o'clock.

❹ It is Friday.

❷ It is December 12.

❺ It is cloudy.

❸ It is ten meters from here to there.

비인칭 주어 it (1)

A Read and match.

① It is sunny.

② It is ten o'clock.

③ It is Friday.

④ It is March 10.

• It is May 15.

• It is very cold.

• It is 8:30 a.m.

• It is Sunday.

B Write the number.

| 4 | It is March 2 today. |

Today is my first day of 4th grade.

| | It is sunny today. |

| | It is 8:00 a.m. My school starts at 9:00. |

| | It takes 10 minutes from home to school. |

 **Color the balloon.**

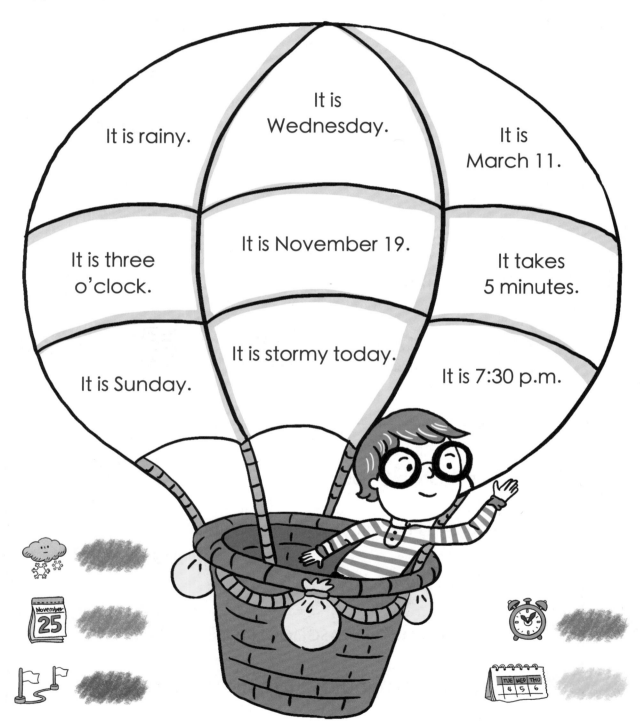

It is rainy.

It is Wednesday.

It is March 11.

It is three o'clock.

It is November 19.

It takes 5 minutes.

It is Sunday.

It is stormy today.

It is 7:30 p.m.

49

비인칭 주어 it (2)

❀ '날씨가 어때?', '무슨 요일이야?'와 같이 비인칭 주어 it을 사용해서 시간,
날씨, 날짜, 요일, 거리 등을 묻고 답할 수 있어요.

[시간]	What time is **it**?	- **It** is 11 o'clock.
[날씨]	How is the weather?	- **It** is sunny today.
[날짜]	What's the date today?	- **It** is May 19.
[요일]	What day is **it**?	- **It** is Saturday today.
[거리]	How far is **it** to the store?	- **It** is 10 miles.

Quick Check-Up

Circle the correct ones.

① **What time is it?**

③ **What day is it?**

② **How far is it?**

④ **How's the weather?**

비인칭 주어 it (2)

A Read and match.

1 What's the date today? •   • It is Sunday.

2 How's the weather?   •   • It takes three hours.

3 How far is it?   •   • It is July 27.

4 What day is it?   •   • It is raining.

5 What time is it?   •   • It is 10:30 a.m.

B Write the number.

1 A: How's the weather?   [1]
   B: It is snowy.

2 A: What time is it?   [   ]
   B: It is10:30 a.m.

3 A: What's the date today?   [   ]
   B: It is November 25.

4 A: What day is it?   [   ]
   B: It is Wednesday.

5 A: How far is it?   [   ]
   B: It is 10 miles.

Read and write the correct one.

Let's go to the park!

It sounds great!

_____ E

It's sunny.

_____

It is 3:00.

_____ from school to the park?

It takes 10 minutes.

_____

It's Thursday.

_____

It's May 4.

A What time is it? **B** How far is it **C** What day is it?

D What's the date today? **E** How is the weather?

· Basic Test ·

A Choose the correct answers.

1 _____ careful.

① Are   ② Be   ③ Is

2 _____ not take the bus.

① Be   ② Does   ③ Do

3 Let's _____ him alone.

① be leaving   ② leaving   ③ leave

4 _____ delicious the noodle is!

① What   ② How often   ③ How

5 _____ a great idea!

① How   ② What   ③ Let's

B Fill in the blanks.

How	It	What	Be

1 _____ fast the cars go!

2 _____ nice to your friends.

3 _____ a little hamster it is!

4 _____ is March 2 today.

C Unscramble the sentences.

1 tell / lie. / Don't / a

_____

2 on the street. / Let's / throw / not / trash

_____

3 How / you / creative / are!

_____

4 old / What / it / is! / computer / an

_____

D Answer the questions.

1 How is the weather today?

_____

2 What time is it now?

_____

3 What day is it today?

_____

4 How far is it from here to your school?

_____

Chapter

과거 시제

11

Lesson 50   Be동사: 과거형

Lesson 51   Be동사 과거 시제: 부정문

Lesson 52   Be동사 과거 시제: 의문문

Lesson 53   일반동사: 과거 시제 1

Lesson 54   일반동사: 과거 시제 2

Lesson 55   일반동사 과거 시제: 부정문

Lesson 56   일반동사 과거 시제: 의문문

Lesson 57   과거 진행형

Lesson 58   과거 진행형: 의문문

I can do it!

Be동사: 과거형

주어의 인칭에 따른 변화

❀ 지나간 일을 나타낼 때에는 동사의 과거 시제를 사용해요. be동사의 과거형은 주어의 인칭과 수에 따라 형태가 달라져요.

주어	be동사 현재	be동사 과거
I	am	was
He, She, It	is	
We, You, They	are	were

I **was** 10 years old last year.
You **were** very tired last night.
He **was** taller than me last year.
They **were** excited that night.

'주어+be동사의 과거형'은 줄여 쓰지 않아요.

Circle the *past be verbs*.

• past be verb 과거형 be동사

❶ I (was) tall and slim.

❷ You were in Paris.

❸ She was a good teacher.

❹ My pet is sick.

❺ He is a singer.

❻ You are so sweet.

❼ I am kind and smart.

❽ He was in the store.

A Look and circle.

① He （was）/ were

② We was / were

③ They was / were

④ It was / were

⑤ She was / were

⑥ I was / were

⑦ You was / were

B Change the sentences in the *past tense*.

① I am in danger. ➡ I was in danger.

② He is excited. ➡ _____

③ They are angry. ➡ _____

④ She is ten years old. ➡ _____

⑤ We are at the zoo. ➡ _____

⑥ It is cold. ➡ _____

 Fun Wrap-Up! **Look and write.**

❶ We ___were___ at the park yesterday.

❷ Judy _____ a singer.

❸ Tom _____ a guitarist.

❹ He _____ beside Judy.

❺ Judy _____ between Tom and Sam.

was

were

Who am I?

I was on the stage yesterday.

I was between Tom and Sam.

I was in the middle of the stage.

Who am I?

I am _____ .

Be동사: 과거형

주어의 수에 따른 변화

✿ be동사 과거 시제의 형태는 주어의 수에 따라서도 다르게 사용해요.

주어			be동사 과거형
단수	this that	**was**	The apple **was** fresh. This **was** green. That **was** yellow.
복수	these those	**were**	The apples **were** delicious. These **were** long. Those **were** short.

✿ [There was+단수명사], [There were+복수명사]는 '〜이 있었다' 라는 의미예요.

There **was** a boy an hour ago.

There **were** many flowers.

Check the correct *past be verbs*.

☑ This was   ☐ Our teachers was

☐ Those was   ☐ You and I were

☐ That was   ☐ I was

☐ These was   ☐ The desk were

☐ His cake were   ☐ His love was

• past be verb 과거형 be동사

A Read and circle.

1 The pencils [was / (were)] on the table.

2 That [was / were] a surprising news.

3 There [was / were] many books in her bag.

4 His brothers and sisters [was / were] in the room.

5 There [was / were] a flower on the ground.

B Fill in the blanks.

was	were

1 We _____ angry yesterday.

2 There _____ a school last month.

Fun Wrap-Up! **Read and write.**

was   were

I __was__ so sad last night.

Me too! I _____ also happy last night.

You _____ happy, not me! Mom and Dad _____ very mean to me.

They _____ always so nice to you. I know.

No, I _____ so hungry, but there _____ no food on the table.

I see. You were hungry last night, but your mom and dad didn't leave any food. So you were sad.

Be동사 과거 시제: 부정문

was not, were not

🌸 be동사 과거의 부정문은 be동사 과거형 뒤에 not을 넣으면 돼요.

	긍정문	부정문
단수	I was excited.	I **was not** excited.
	You were in Paris.	You **were not** in Paris.
	He was happy.	He **was not** happy.
	She was kind.	She **was not** kind.
	It was long.	It **was not** long.
	There was a book.	There **was not** a book.
복수	We were at the zoo.	We **were not** at the zoo.
	You were students.	You **were not** students.
	They were friends.	They **were not** friends.
	There were children.	There **were not** children.

Quick Check-Up — Check the correct ones.

☑ He was not happy.　　☐ That not was a great movie.

☐ I not was a teacher.　　☐ There were not books.

☐ She was not cute.　　☐ He were not kind.

☐ It were not long.　　☐ They were not teachers.

was not, were not

A Complete the *negative forms*.

1. These fruits ___were not fresh___. (were fresh)

2. The boy _____. (was in the room)

3. The TV show _____. (was interesting)

4. They _____. (were happy)

5. He _____. (was my uncle)

B Unscramble the sentences.

1. The books / not / good stories. / were

   ___The books were not good stories.___

2. not / a good singer. / She / was

   _____

3. closed / The stores / not / were / yesterday.

   _____

4. doctors / We / not / were / last year.

   _____

was not, were not

 **Choose and draw.**

☐ I was not happy last night, but I am happy now.

☐ I was not hungry, but I am hungry now.

☐ It was rainy yesterday, but it is sunny today.

Be동사 과거 시제: 부정문

wasn't, weren't

❀ was not, were not은 각각 wasn't, weren't로 줄일 수 있어요.

	부정문	축약형
단수	I **was not** excited.	I **wasn't** excited.
	You **were not** in Paris.	You **weren't** in Paris.
	He **was not** happy.	He **wasn't** happy.
	She **was not** kind.	She **wasn't** kind.
	It **was not** long.	It **wasn't** long.
	There **was not** a book.	There **wasn't** a book.
복수	We **were not** at the zoo.	We **weren't** at the zoo.
	You **were not** students.	You **weren't** students.
	They **were not** friends.	They **weren't** friends.
	There **were not** children.	There **weren't** children.

Quick Check-Up Check the correct *short forms*. • short form 축약형

☑ I wasn't at home.   ☐ It was't boring.

☐ There weren't pencils.   ☐ The food wasn't fresh.

☐ She wasnot tall.   ☐ He weren't kind.

☐ There weren't a book.   ☐ We weren't surprised.

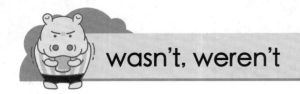

wasn't, weren't

A Read and mark ○ or ✕.

1. You weren't happy. ⬭⬭⬭⬭⬭⬭⬭⬭⬭⬭⬭⬭ ○

2. There wasn't a book. ⬭⬭⬭⬭⬭⬭⬭⬭

3. I wasn't in a hurry. ⬭⬭⬭⬭⬭⬭⬭⬭⬭

4. There weren't enough food. ⬭⬭⬭⬭

5. All schools weren't open. ⬭⬭⬭⬭⬭⬭

B Change the sentences in their *negative short forms*.

1. The juice was fresh.

   The juice wasn't fresh.

2. There was Mom in the living room.

   _____

3. I was taller than you.

   _____

4. There were two tables in the living room.

   _____

 Match and color.

wasn't   weren't

It

We

You

They

wasn't

weren't

He

You

She

Be동사 과거 시제: 의문문

질문하기

❀ be동사 과거 의문문: [Was / Were + 주어 ~?]

	긍정문	의문문
단수	I was happy.	**Was I** happy**?**
	You were tired.	**Were you** tired**?**
	He was a teacher.	**Was he** a teacher**?**
	She was strong.	**Was she** strong**?**
	It was a good story.	**Was it** a good story**?**
	There was a book in the bag.	**Was there** a book in the bag**?**
복수	We were good teachers.	**Were we** good teachers**?**
	You were in London.	**Were you** in London**?**
	They were at the zoo.	**Were they** at the zoo**?**
	There were many cars.	**Were there** many cars**?**

Quick Check-Up Circle the correct ones.

① ⟨Was⟩ / Were he a doctor?

② Was / Were the apples on the table?

③ Was / Were the movie fun last night?

④ Was / Were your mom angry yesterday?

A Make the *asking sentences*.

1 We were at the museum.   Were we at the museum?

2 There were many books.   _____

3 The tickets were expensive.   _____

4 The zoo was crowded.   _____

5 It was a happy day.   _____

B Unscramble the sentences.

1 you / 10 years old / two years ago? / Were

Were you 10 years old two years ago?

2 Was / a good / your partner / driver?

_____

3 on the table? / Was / there / a spoon

_____

 Check the correct ones.

✓ Was she hungry?	Was they at home?	Was he a doctor?	Was this a mouse?
Were you strangers?	Was there 10 books?	Was the movie fun?	Was it sweet?
Was they happy?	Were there sugar?	Were you excited?	Was we happy?
Was this cute?	Were those flowers?	Was that a bird?	Were you at home?

Be동사 과거 시제: 의문문

대답하기

✿ be동사 과거형으로 시작하는 의문문에 대한 대답은 다음과 같이 해요.

	의문문	긍정 대답	부정 대답
단수	**Was I** happy**?**	Yes, you **were**.	No, you **were not/weren't**.
	Were you tired**?**	Yes, I **was**.	No, I **was not/wasn't**.
	Was he a teacher**?**	Yes, he **was**.	No, he **was not/wasn't**.
	Was she strong**?**	Yes, she **was**.	No, she **was not/wasn't**.
	Was it a good story**?**	Yes, it **was**.	No, it **was not/wasn't**.
	Was there a book**?**	Yes, there **was**.	No, there **was not/wasn't**.
복수	**Were we** good teachers**?**	Yes, you **were**.	No, you **were not/weren't**.
	Were you in London**?**	Yes, we **were**.	No, we **were not/weren't**.
	Were they at school**?**	Yes, they **were**.	No, they **were not/weren't**.
	Were there many cars**?**	Yes, there **were**.	No, there **were not/weren't**.

Quick Check-Up

Check the correct answers.

❶ Was he a student?

☑ Yes, he was

☐ Yes, I was.

❸ Were your sisters angry?

☐ Yes, they weren't.

☐ Yes, they were.

❷ Were you a teacher?

☐ Yes, I were.

☐ No, I wasn't.

❹ Was there a cat?

☐ Yes, there were.

☐ No, there wasn't.

대답하기

A Read and match.

1 Was there a book?   •   • Yes, you were.

2 Were you excited?   •   • No, she wasn't.

3 Were we in danger?   •   • No, it wasn't.

4 Was she happy?   •   • No, I wasn't.

5 Was it his bag?   •   • Yes, there was.

B Answer the questions.

1 Was John sad?

<u>Yes, he was.</u>

2 Were they at the zoo?

_____

3 Was there a book on the table?

_____

Cut and paste.

※ 아래와 동일한 전개도가 169쪽에 있습니다. 해당 페이지의 전개도를 사용하세요.

Q: Were you a singer?

A: Yes, I was.

Q: Was the boy happy?

A: No, he wasn't. He was sad.

Q: Was there the sun?

A: Yes, there was.

Q: Was there a flower in the bottle?

A: No, there wasn't.

Q: Were they happy?

A: Yes, they were.

Q: Were there toys in the box?

A: Yes, there were.

Go to p. 169

일반동사: 과거 시제 1

규칙 변화 (1)

❀ 일반동사의 과거는 과거의 동작이나 행동을 나타내요. 대부분의 일반동사 과거형은 '동사원형-(e)d'로 표현해요.

yesterday	today
과거	현재
동사-(e)d	동사원형/동사-(e)s
I watch**ed** TV last night.	I watch TV.
She talk**ed** to me yesterday.	She talk**s** to me.

❀ 과거 시제는 일반적으로 과거의 때를 나타내는 말들과 같이 쓰여요.
 ex yesterday, last night, last week, last year, two years ago...

❀ 역사적 사실을 말할 때는 항상 과거 시제를 사용해요.

Quick Check-Up

Circle the correct *tense*.

• tense 시제

❶ I open my eyes.　　　　　　　　(present)/ past

❷ I talked to Mom.　　　　　　　　present / past

❸ The baby speaks funny words.　　present / past

❹ They called me last night.　　　　present / past

❺ Mom and Dad loved me.　　　　present / past

규칙 변화 (1)

A Circle the correct ones.

1. I [play / (played)] soccer last night.

2. They [watch / watched] TV yesterday.

3. Babies [jump / jumped] on the bed one hour ago.

4. The lady [opens / opened] the door yesterday.

5. I [clean / cleaned] my room last night.

B Change the sentences.

| Present Simple | ➡ | Past Simple |

1. I brush my teeth. ➡ I __brushed__ my teeth.

2. I wash my face. ➡ I _____ my face.

3. Mom talks to me. ➡ Mom _____ to me.

4. Dad loves me. ➡ Dad _____ me.

5. We laugh out loud. ➡ We _____ out loud.

 Color the leaves.

past simple   present simple

We watched the movie.

They dance.

She wants a bird.

Mom played tennis.

Tom washed the dishes last night.

He rides a bike.

I brushed my teeth.

일반동사: 과거 시제 1

규칙 변화 (2)

❀ 일반동사의 과거형은 아래와 같은 규칙들로 만들어요.

대부분의 동사	-ed	play - played look - looked	brush - brushed jump - jumped
e로 끝나는 동사	-d	dance - danced love - loved	like - liked move - moved
[자음+y]로 끝나는 동사	y → -ied	dry - dried study - studied	try - tried worry - worried
[단모음+단자음]으로 끝나는 동사	자음을 한 번 더 쓰고 + ed	plan - planned stop - stopped	rub - rubbed drop - dropped

Circle the correct ones.

❶ I
(dried)
dryed
my hair one hour ago.

❷ The girl
dropped
droped
her ice cream.

❸ He
rubed
rubbed
his tummy.

A Write the present tense verbs in the *past tense* ones.

1. He finishes the book yesterday.   finished

2. I stay at the library last night.   _____

3. Tom moves to a new house yesterday.   _____

4. Max stops his car.   _____

5. The baby cries 10 minutes ago.   _____

6. I love my family.   _____

B Correct and rewrite.

1. He **planed** his summer vacation.   planned

2. She **tryed** to open the heavy door.   _____

3. They **danceed** happily.   _____

4. She **enjoied** the movie.   _____

5. We **liveed** in that house one year ago.   _____

Follow the right sentences.

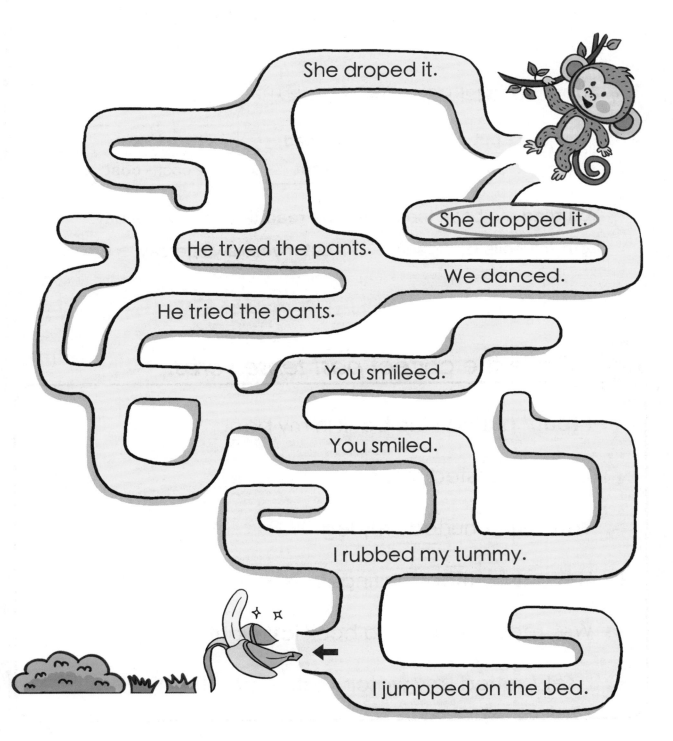

She droped it.

She dropped it.

He tryed the pants.

We danced.

He tried the pants.

You smileed.

You smiled.

I rubbed my tummy.

I jumped on the bed.

일반동사: 과거 시제 2

불규칙 변화 (1)

❁ 대부분의 일반동사는 동사원형에 -ed를 붙여서 과거형을 만들어요.
하지만 어떤 동사들은 -ed를 붙이지 않는데 이런 동사를 '불규칙 동사'라고 해요.

❁ 현재형과 과거형의 모양이 같은 불규칙 동사

put - **put**	read - **read**	set - **set**
hit - **hit**	cut - **cut**	cost - **cost**

You **read** the book today. → You **read** the book yesterday.

I **cut** my nails by myself. → I **cut** my nails yesterday.

Quick Check-Up

Circle the correct *past tense verbs*.

❶ I [put / putted] the book in my bag.

❷ It [cost / costed] a lot.

❸ You [hurt / hurted] my leg.

❹ He [cut / cutted] his finger.

❺ We [read / readed] a book last night.

❻ I [set / setted] my watch yesterday.

• past tense verb 과거 시제 동사

불규칙 변화 (1)

A Circle the correct *tense*.

1. She hurt her leg two days ago.
present / ⃝past

2. She puts down the cake.
present / past

3. Mom read a book last night.
present / past

4. I set the table for Mom yesterday.
present / past

5. The ticket cost $15 last night.
present / past

B Fill in the blanks.

set	hurt	cost	read	hit

1. The meal ___cost___ me $10 last month.

2. He _____ his watch yesterday.

3. I _____ my knee yesterday.

4. My friend _____ the book last week.

5. She _____ the ball.

 Cut and put.

※ 아래와 동일한 카드가 167쪽에 있습니다. 해당 페이지의 카드를 사용하세요.

put	read	play	cut	hurt
cost	talk	hit	walk	jump

Go to p. 167

불규칙 변화 (2)

✿ 현재형과 형태가 다른 불규칙 동사

bring - **brought**	feel - **felt**	lose - **lost**	sit - **sat**
build - **built**	find - **found**	make - **made**	sleep - **slept**
buy - **bought**	fly - **flew**	meet - **met**	speak - **spoke**
come - **came**	get - **got**	pay - **paid**	stand - **stood**
do - **did**	give - **gave**	run - **ran**	swim - **swam**
draw - **drew**	go - **went**	say - **said**	take - **took**
drink - **drank**	have - **had**	see - **saw**	tell - **told**
drive - **drove**	hear - **heard**	sell - **sold**	think - **thought**
eat - **ate**	know - **knew**	sing - **sang**	write - **wrote**

172쪽에 동사 변화표가 있으니
꼭 외워두도록 해요.

Quick Check-Up Circle the correct ones.

❶

swimed
(swam)

❷

drank
drinked

❸

singed
sang

❹

runed
ran

A Write the *past tense form* of the word.

1 Dave ___ate___ a slice of pizza. (eat)

2 They _____ on the bench. (sit)

3 He _____ a fairy tale to his children. (tell)

4 The man _____ a robot. (make)

5 They _____ to the zoo. (go)

B Circle the correct ones.

1 I drawed / (drew) pictures last night.

2 Mom buyed / bought some books.

3 The boy sleeped / slept on the bed.

4 She gived / gave me a gift.

5 I heared / heard a noise.

6 The cats runned / ran fast.

Fun Wrap-Up! Complete the puzzle.

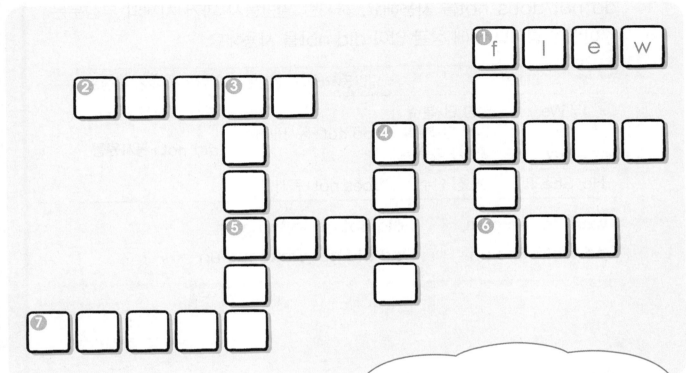

① f l e w

Change the given words to their irregular *past tense verbs*.

Across	Down
① fly	① find
② write	③ teach
④ buy	④ blow
⑤ give	
⑥ do	
⑦ sleep	

일반동사 과거 시제: 부정문

did not

✿ 일반동사 현재 시제의 부정문은 주어의 인칭이나 수에 따라
do not/does not을 사용해요. 하지만 일반동사 과거 시제의 부정문은
주어의 인칭이나 수에 상관 없이 **did not**을 사용해요.

주어		일반동사 현재 부정문	일반동사 과거 부정문
I / We You They	1인칭 단·복수 2인칭 단·복수 3인칭 복수	do not+동사원형	**did not**+**동사원형**
He, She, It	3인칭 단수	does not+동사원형	

I **went** to the gym. → I **did not go** to the gym.

Dad **woke** me up. → Dad **did not wake** me up.

Quick Check-Up — Check the correct position for *did not*.

① The boy _____ ✔ _____ tell me _____ the story.

② I _____ have _____ time.

③ We _____ play _____ in the park.

④ They _____ hit _____ the ball.

⑤ He _____ give _____ me a book.

did not

A Complete the sentences in their *negative forms*.

1 They _____did not eat_____ lunch at the cafe. (ate)

2 I _____ TV yesterday. (watched)

3 She _____ the door. (opened)

4 Susan _____ the movie. (liked)

5 Mom _____ me money. (gave)

B Unscramble the sentences.

1 did not / put on / Jane / a shirt.

_____Jane did not put on a shirt._____

2 They / cut / did not / the ribbon.

_____

3 You / paint / did not / the wall.

_____

 Fun Wrap-Up! Look, read, and circle.

He jumped.	She ran.	She danced.	She swam.
(He did not jump.)	She did not run.	She did not dance.	She did not swim.

일반동사 과거 시제: 부정문

didn't

❋ did not은 didn't로 줄여 쓰기도 해요.

I **did not** open the door.
=didn't

You **did not** study English.
=didn't

We **did not** leave for London.
=didn't

She **did not** eat pizza.
=didn't

They **did not** sit on the bench.
=didn't

I **did not** play the piano.
=didn't

You **did not** swim in the lake.
=didn't

We **did not** buy anything.
=didn't

He **did not** hit the ball.
=didn't

They **did not** fight.
=didn't

Quick Check-Up
Check the correct position for *didn't*.

❶ She ____✓____ study _____ English.

❷ Sam _____ read _____ the books.

❸ I _____ play _____ the piano yesterday.

❹ Dad _____ drive _____ a car.

❺ We _____ watch _____ the movie.

❻ The students _____ sing _____ a song for us.

 **didn't**

A Correct and rewrite.

① I didn't ~~forgot~~ my book.   _forget_

② The singers didn't **arrived** late.   _____

③ She didn't **traveled** to London.   _____

④ He didn't **danced** yesterday.   _____

⑤ We didn't **watched** the film.   _____

B Complete the *negative form* with *didn't*.

① She ___didn't answer___ the phone. (answered)

② She _____ the festival. (enjoyed)

③ I _____ with my friends. (played)

④ I _____ the vases. (washed)

⑤ They _____ my room. (cleaned)

Fun Wrap-Up! **Follow the correct *negative sentences*.**

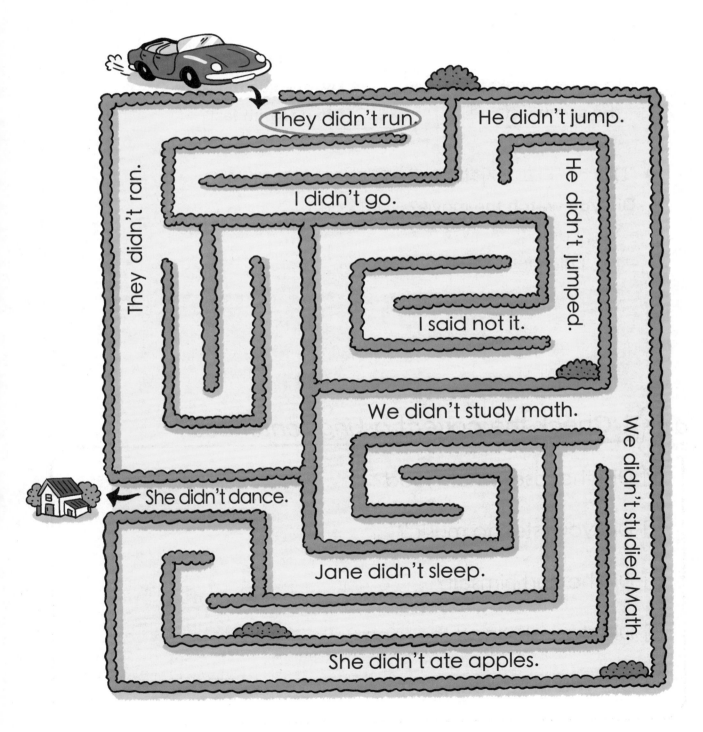

They didn't run.

He didn't jump.

They didn't ran.

I didn't go.

He didn't jumped.

I said not it.

We didn't study math.

She didn't dance.

We didn't studied Math.

Jane didn't sleep.

She didn't ate apples.

일반동사 과거 시제: 의문문

Did ~?

❀ 일반동사 과거형의 의문문은 [Did+주어+동사원형 ~?]의 형태로 만들어요.

평서문	의문문
They **left** the hotel.	**Did** they **leave** the hotel**?**
She **saw** monkeys.	**Did** she **see** monkeys**?**
He **swam** fast.	**Did** he **swim** fast**?**

❀ "Did ~?"라고 과거형으로 물으면 다음과 같이 대답해요.

Did you watch the movie?

– Yes, I did.

– No, I didn't(=did not).

Quick Check-Up — Check the correct *asking sentences*.

☑ Did the roses smell good?

☐ Did you listen to music?

☐ Did he hurt himself?

☐ Did they cleaned the room?

☐ Did you liked your puppy?

• asking sentence 의문문

Did ~?

A Change the sentences into the *asking sentences*.

1 Tim set the table last night. (set - set)

➡. Did Tim set the table last night?

2 The young lady slept on the bed. (sleep - slept)

➡ _____

3 Hanna drove the car to the store. (drive - drove)

➡ _____

B Circle the correct ones.

1 Did you finished / (finish) the book?

2 Did you played / play soccer?

3 Did you hear the story?
  - Yes, I did / do .

4 Did they know each other?
  - No, they didn't / weren't .

Did ~?

 **Look and answer.**

| Yes, they did. | Yes, he did. | Yes, she did. |
| No, they didn't. | No, he didn't. | No, she didn't. |

1 Did the family go to the zoo?   Yes, they did.

2 Did they see tigers at the zoo?

3 Did the man carry a bag?

4 Did the boy wear a cap?

5 Did the girl wear glasses?

의문사+did ~?

✿ 의문사가 있는 일반동사 과거 시제 의문문은

[의문사+**did**+주어+동사원형 ~?]의 형태로 만들어요.

Who, When,
Where, What,
Why, How

I, you, we,
he, she, it,
they...

✿ 의문사가 있는 의문문은 yes/no로 대답하지 않고 구체적으로 답해요.

Where did they go?

– They went **to the museum**.

What did you do yesterday?

– I did **my homework**.

Circle the correct ones.

① Where (did) / do you go yesterday?

② What did / were you do last night?

③ When did / was he call me?

④ Why did / do the baby cry last night?

⑤ Who did / were you see?

의문사+did ~?

Ⓐ Read and match.

1. When did you get up? •   • Grandpa.

2. Where did she go? •   • By bus.

3. How did Tom get there? •   • At 6:30 a.m.

4. Who did you visit? •   • English.

5. What did she teach? •   • To Paris.

Ⓑ Unscramble the sentences.

1. did / When / she / meet / her friends?

   When did she meet her friends?

2. you / did / cry / Why / last night?

   _____

3. did / go / Where / they / after school?

   _____

Fun Wrap-Up! ## Look and answer.

Mom, I feel great!

A cap.	He felt great.	Two tigers.
A mobile phone.	They went to the zoo.	

1 Where did the family go?   They went to the zoo.

2 What did they see at the zoo?   _____

3 What did the man hold in his hands?   _____

4 What did the boy wear on his head?   _____

5 How did the boy feel?   _____

긍정문

❀ '～하고 있는 중이었다'라고 과거의 어느 시점에 진행 중이었던 일을 표현하고 싶을 때 과거 진행형을 써요.

과거 진행형은 [was/were + 동사원형 -ing]로 나타내요.

I **was reading** a book.　　　　They **were dancing** at the party.

❀ 과거 진행형의 '동사원형 -ing' 형태는 다음과 같이 만들어요.

대부분의 동사	eat - eat**ing**	go - go**ing**	walk - walk**ing**
e로 끝나는 동사	write - writ**ing**	make - mak**ing**	come - com**ing**
ie로 끝나는 동사	lie - l**ying**	die - d**ying**	tie - t**ying**
[단모음+단자음]으로 끝나는 동사	put - put**ting**	run - run**ning**	swim - swim**ming**

Quick Check-Up Check the correct ones.

☑ Steve and Sally were singing.

☐ We was eating some ice cream.

☐ I were reading a book.

☐ You were listening to music.

☐ She is talking on the phone yesterday.

긍정문

A Choose the correct ones.

1 She （was／ were） reading a book.

2 The bees was / were buzzing.

3 He was / were playing soccer.

4 We was / were dancing.

5 Tom and Marry was / were walking on the street.

B Complete the *past continuous sentences*.

1 They ___were swimming___ . (swim)

2 He _____ on the couch. (sleep)

3 We _____ breakfast. (have)

4 Sara _____ the fence. (paint)

5 I _____ my hands. (wash)

 **Write the *past continuous sentences*.**

When you visited us...

➊ Dad _____ lunch. (cook)

➋ Mom _____ a book. (read)

➌ Grandpa _____ a nap on the couch. (take)

➍ Grandma _____ a cup of coffee. (drink)

부정문

❀ 과거 진행형의 부정문은 과거의 어느 시점에 '무엇을 하고 있는 중이 아니었다'라고 말할 때 사용하며 [was/were+not+동사원형-ing] 형태로 나타내요.

I **was not playing** tennis.

He **was not sleeping** in his room.

She **was not talking** on the phone.

We **were not drawing** on the walls.

❀ was not은 wasn't로, were not은 weren't로 줄여 쓸 수 있어요.

I **was not**(=**wasn't**) playing tennis.

They **were not**(=**weren't**) swimming.

Quick Check-Up Check the correct position for *not*.

❶ She ___ was ✔ reading ___ a book.

❷ ___ The students ___ were ___ singing.

❸ I ___ was ___ playing ___ the guitar.

❹ ___ You were ___ reading ___ a newspaper.

❺ ___ Mom ___ was ___ working on the computer.

❻ I was ___ looking ___ at ___ you.

A Complete the sentences.

1 I ___wasn't___ dancing. I was reading books.

2 Jim _____ singing songs in the concert.
He was playing the violin.

3 I _____ knocking on the door,
but you didn't hear it.

wasn't

was

B Describe the pictures.

1  Jack was not answering the phone.
He _____ his hair. (dry)

2 Tom wasn't watching TV.
He _____ a book. (read)

3  Jane wasn't eating a banana.
She _____ an apple. (eat)

 **Fun Wrap-Up!** # Find the way to your friend.

Cats was eating their food.

He wasn't running.

I was not singing.

I wasn't planting seeds.

It weren't running.

Start

It were not raining.

She was dancing.

I wasn't swimming.

The frog was hopping.

과거 진행형: 의문문

yes/no 의문문

❀ 과거 진행형 의문문은 과거의 어느 시점에 무엇을 하고 있었는지 물어 볼 때 사용해요. 형태는 [Was/Were+주어+동사원형 -ing ~?]로 나타내요.

She was dancing on the floor.　**They were** talking about football.

Was she dancing on the floor?　**Were they** talking about football?

❀ Was/Were로 시작하는 과거 진행형 의문문은 다음과 같이 대답해요.

Was she doing her homework?　**Were you** singing on the stage?

– Yes, she was.　　　　　　　　　　　– Yes, we were.

– No, she wasn't.　　　　　　　　　　– No, we weren't.

Quick Check-Up Check the correct *asking sentences*.

☑ Was he singing a song?

☐ Were you sleeping now?

☐ Were you read the book?

☐ You was pointing at the bananas?

☐ Were they climbing the mountains?

• asking sentence 의문문

yes/no 의문문

A Change the sentences into the *asking sentences*.

① She was looking at the flowers.

➡ Was she looking at the flowers?

② Tom was having breakfast.

➡ _____

③ He was thinking about the plan.

➡ _____

④ They were looking into the mirror.

➡ _____

B Answer the questions.

① Was he crying?

- _____

② Was she feeding birds?

- _____

yes/no 의문문

Fun Wrap-Up! **Read the sentences and write the right number.**

1

_____

_____

_____

① Were they watching TV?
   - Yes, they were.

② Was he playing with his toys?
   - Yes, he was.

③ Was he listening to music?
   - No, he was studying math.

과거 진행형: 의문문

의문사 있는 의문문

❋ who, what, when, where, how, why 등의 의문사를 사용해서 과거 진행형 의문문을 만들 수 있어요.

[의문사+was/were+주어+동사원형-ing ~?] 형태로 나타내고, 대답을 할 때에는 yes/no가 아니라 구체적으로 답해야 해요.

What was he doing?

– He was **talking on the phone**.

Where were they going?

– They were going **to the hospital**.

Who was reading a book?

– **John** was reading a book.

Check the correct answers.

❶ Where were you going?

☑ To the hospital.

☐ Yes, I was.

❸ What were they doing?

☐ Homework.

☐ No, they weren't.

❷ Who was running?

☐ Jane.

☐ To the market.

❹ Why was she crying?

☐ She cut her fingers.

☐ Yes, she was.

A Unscramble the sentences.

1 were / Why / reading / you / books?

Why were you reading books?

2 When / they / listening to music? / were

_____

3 Where / she / was / going?

_____

4 he / eating? / What / was

_____

B Read and mark ○ or ✕.

1 What were you doing?

  - I was running. ⬚⬚⬚⬚⬚⬚⬚⬚⬚ ○

2 Who were you talking to?

  - Yes, I was. ⬚⬚⬚⬚⬚⬚⬚⬚⬚ ☐

3 When were they listening to music?

  - At 7:00 p.m. ⬚⬚⬚⬚⬚⬚⬚⬚⬚ ☐

Answer the questions.

	Steve	Jane
Friday	ride a bike	sing a song
Saturday	fly a kite	play baseball

1 What was Steve doing on Friday?

He was riding a bike.

2 When was Jane playing baseball?

_____

3 Who was flying a kite?

_____

· Basic Test ·

A Choose the correct answers.

1   Babies _____ on the bed one hour ago.

    ① jump   ② jumps   ③ jumped

2   I _____ a noise.

    ① heared   ② heard   ③ hears

3   Susan _____ the movie.

    ① didn't like   ② didn't liked   ③ doesn't liked

4   Where were you going? - _____

    ① Yes, I was.   ② No, I wasn't.   ③ To the hospital.

5   When did you get up? - _____

    ① By bus.   ② At 6:30 a.m.   ③ To Paris.

B Fill in the blanks.

were	told	Was	was

1   He _____ a fairy tale to his children.

2   Who _____ running?

3   _____ the movie fun last night?

4   They _____ talking about football.

C Unscramble the sentences.

1 Were / expensive? / the tickets

_____

2 He / was / me / taller than / last year.

_____

3 yesterday. / closed / were / not / The stores

_____

4 Were / looking / they / into the mirror?

_____

D Answer the questions.

1 How old were you last year?

_____

2 What did you do yesterday?

_____

3 What did you eat for breakfast today?

_____

4 Did you cut your nails yesterday?

_____

Chapter

미래 시제

12

Lesson 59 미래 시제

Lesson 60 미래 시제: 의문문

I can do it!

미래 시제

will

❀ 앞으로 일어날 일을 말하거나 예측할 때에는 미래 시제를 써서 표현해요. 미래 시제는 [will+동사원형]의 형태로 나타내며 '~일 것이다, ~할 것이다'라고 해석해요.

I **will visit** my parents next Sunday.
They **will be** back to school next August.

❀ 주어가 I, you, she처럼 인칭대명사일 경우, 다음과 같이 줄여 쓸 수 있어요.
I'll visit my parents next Sunday.
They'll be back to school next August.

❀ will의 부정형은 [will+not+동사원형]으로 나타내며, will not은 won't 로 줄여 쓸 수 있어요.
I **will not**(=**won't**) visit my parents next Sunday.

Quick Check-Up — Check the correct place for *will*.

① He __✓__ be ___ a soccer player ___ .

② ___ She ___ play ___ tennis tomorrow.

③ I ___ not ___ drive my car to ___ the school.

will

A Use *will* to complete the sentences.

1. I _____will finish_____ the book by 5 p.m. (finish)

2. I _____ a firefighter in the future. (be)

3. They _____ in the garden tomorrow. (work)

4. I _____ the window. (open)

5. It _____ this weekend. (rain)

B Correct and rewrite.

1. I **buy** a new pen tomorrow. _____

2. She **is** ten years old next year. _____will be_____

3. I **go** to the beach soon. _____

4. I **get up** early tomorrow morning. _____

5. He **watches** the movie next Sunday. _____

6. They **played** basketball next weekend. _____

 **Look and write.**

Kate, what will you do this Saturday?

10:00 a.m.	2:00 p.m.	5:00 p.m.	8:00 p.m.

① I _____will have breakfast_____ at 10:00 a.m.
(have breakfast)

② I _____ at 2:00 p.m.
(play baseball)

③ I _____ at 5:00 p.m.
(read a book)

④ I _____ at 8:00 p.m.
(watch TV)

미래 시제

be going to

✿ 미리 계획해 둔 미래의 일을 나타낼 때에는 [be going to+동사원형]의 형태를 써요.

I **am going to** wash my car this Sunday.

He **is going to** play the guitar this afternoon.

✿ be going to의 부정형은 [be동사+not going to+동사원형] 형태로 표현하며, '~하지 않을 것이다'라는 뜻으로 사용해요.

I **am not going to** meet my friends tomorrow.

She **is not going to** come home this weekend.

✿ will과 be going to는 미래를 나타내는 다음과 같은 표현들과 자주 쓰여요.

tomorrow, soon, later, in the future, next week, next month,

in two years, in one hour...

Quick Check-Up

Mark △ or O.

| △ future time words | ◎ past time words |

☐ tomorrow　　☐ next month　　☐ yesterday

△ in three years　　◎ last night　　☐ two years later

☐ soon　　☐ last Sunday　　☐ three hours ago

☐ next week　　☐ in the future　　☐ next Saturday

be going to

A Complete the sentences. Use *be going to*.

1 We ___are going to clean___ the room. (clean)

2 We _____ TV tomorrow evening. (watch)

3 They _____ next week. (go fishing)

4 I _____ a storybook later. (read)

5 I _____ the mountain tomorrow. (climb)

B Unscramble the sentences.

1 is going to / My son / play basketball / tomorrow.

___My son is going to play basketball tomorrow.___

2 visit / He / this summer. / is going to / his cousin

_____

3 I'm / study / going to / English / this weekend.

_____

 **Fun Wrap-Up!** # What are the children going to do tomorrow?

1 Amy ___is going to visit___ her grandma. (visit)

2 Tom _____ soccer. (play)

3 Jack _____ a book. (read)

4 Janet _____. (swim)

5 Hera _____ the mountains with her friend. (climb)

미래 시제: 의문문

will 의문문

❀ 미래 시제 will 의문문은 [Will+주어+동사원형 ~?]의 형태로 물어 보고 대답은 [Yes, 주어+will.] 또는 [No, 주어+will not(=won't).]로 답해요.

Will she play basketball tomorrow?

– Yes, she will.

– No, she will not(=won't).

❀ 의문사로 시작하는 will 의문문은 [의문사+will+주어+동사원형 ~?]으로 나타내요.

What will you do this Friday?   **When will** he visit us?

– I will stay at home.   – Probably 8 p.m.

Quick Check-Up Circle the correct ones.

❶ Will you go / going to the store?

❷ Will they eating / eat pizza for lunch?

❸ What will you do / did after school?

❹ Will David invites / invite us to his party?

❺ Will Tom and Jane sing / singing a song?

❻ What time will he visits / visit us?

 **will 의문문**

A Unscramble the sentences.

① you / Will / go fishing?   <u>Will you go fishing?</u>

② buy the pen? / she / Will   _____

③ they / Will / take a taxi?   _____

④ do / on Sunday? / will / What / you

_____

⑤ will / you / When / go shopping?

_____

B Choose and circle.

① What will Tom and Suzy do tomorrow?

- They ⟨will have⟩/ have a party.

② When will he meet her?

- He meets / will meet her next month.

③ Will they play baseball tomorrow?

- No, they will / they won't .

will 의문문

 **Read and write.**

Tom's Plan

I will get up early in the morning.

I will play tennis for my health.

I will study English for an hour every day.

I will visit Grandma every weekend.

1 Will Tom get up early in the morning?

Yes, he will.

2 What will he do for his health?

3 Will he study English for two hours every day?

4 Who will he visit every weekend?

be going to 의문문

❋ be going to 의문문은 [be동사＋주어＋going to＋동사원형 ～?]의 형태로 묻고, 대답은 [Yes, 주어＋be동사.] 또는 [No, 주어＋be동사＋not.] 으로 답해요.

Is he **going to** travel to London?

– Yes, he is.

– No, he is not(＝isn't).

❋ 의문사가 있는 be going to 의문문은
[의문사＋be동사＋주어＋going to＋동사원형 ～?]으로 나타내요.

What are you **going to** do tomorrow**?**

– I'm going to stay at home.

Who are they **going to** visit**?**

– They are going to visit their mom.

Circle the correct ones.

① (Are)/ Will you going to ride this bike?

② Is / Are you going to stay at home?

③ Are / Is he going to paint the walls?

④ Will / Is John going to fix his toy car?

⑤ Is / Are they going to go fishing?

be going to 의문문

A Unscramble the sentences.

1 you / going to / study English / Are / tomorrow?

Are you going to study English tomorrow?

2 are / you / going to / What time / get up?

_____

3 are / you / When / going to / go to bed / tonight?

_____

4 going to / are / you / What / eat for lunch?

_____

B Answer the questions.

1 Are you going to have lunch now?

- No, I am not / am . I am going to have a rest.

2 Is he going to buy a new toy?

- Yes, he isn't / is . He's going to buys / buy one.

3 Are they going to wash the car tomorrow?

- Yes / No , they aren't. They're going to fix / fixes it.

Fun Wrap-Up! Ask and answer.

Is he going to study?

Are you going to swim?

What are you going to do?

What is she going to do?

(swim)

_____

(play soccer)

_____

(play with toys)

No, he isn't.

(read a book)

_____

· Basic Test ·

A Choose the correct answers.

1   I _____ read a storybook later.
    ① are going to   ② am going to   ③ is going to

2   We _____ clean the room.
    ① is going to   ② are going to   ③ am going to

3   He will meet her _____.
    ① next month   ② yesterday   ③ last weekend

4   What will Tom and Suzy do _____?
    ① last month   ② tomorrow   ③ two hours ago

5   Will they play baseball tomorrow? - No, _____.
    ① they were   ② they will   ③ they won't

B Fill in the blanks.

| are you   will open   this weekend   wash |

1   She is not going to come home _____.

2   I _____ the window.

3   Are they going to _____ the car tomorrow?

4   When _____ going to go to bed tonight?

C Unscramble the sentences.

1 will / rain / It / this weekend.

_____

2 Amy / visit / is going to / her grandma.

_____

3 When / you / go fishing? / will

_____

4 are / you / do / What / going to / tomorrow?

_____

D Answer the questions.

1 What are you going to do today?

_____

2 What are you going to do tomorrow?

_____

3 When will you get up tomorrow?

_____

4 What are you going to do this weekend?

_____

MEMO

Answers

의문사의 종류

p. 6

Quick Check-Up

☑ who ☑ how ☑ why
☐ because ☐ then ☐ however
☐ they ☑ where ☑ when
☐ there ☐ so ☑ what

A p. 7

1. (When) / Where is your birthday?
2. (How) / Who can you make it?
3. (What) / When do you like?
4. Why / (Who) is your best friend?
5. (How) / What are you today?

B p. 7

1. __What__ is his name? — It's John.
2. __When__ is her birthday? — It's on June 3.
3. __Where__ does John live? — He lives in Seoul.
4. __How__ is your teacher? — He is good.
5. __Why__ are you late? — I missed the train.

Fun Wrap-Up! p. 8

Who is that man? - It's Tom's dad.
Where is my watch? - It's on the table.
What is he doing? - He is working.
When does he come? - This afternoon.
How are you? - I'm good.
Why are you happy? - Because I found my cat.

의문사 있는 의문문

p. 9

Quick Check-Up

1. (What does he) / What he does want?
2. Is where / (Where is) my pen?
3. Why (is it) / it is so hot?
4. Why (do you) / you do swim?

A p. 10

1. do / Why / study math? / you
   __Why do you study math?__

2. you / do / When / go to bed?
   __When do you go to bed?__

3. feel? / you / How / do
   __How do you feel?__

B p. 10

1. __Where__ __does__ she live? — She lives in Busan.
2. __Why__ __do__ you cry? — Because the movie is sad.
3. __When__ __is__ your birthday? — It is on March 5.
4. __Why__ __does__ he need a fan? — Because it's very hot.
5. __How__ __do__ you feel? — I feel great.

Fun Wrap-Up! p. 11

1. Where is Sam? — __He is in front of the bushes.__
2. Who drinks juice? — __Amy (drinks juice).__
3. What does Suzy eat? — __A sandwich. /She eats a sandwich.__

의문대명사

p. 12

Quick Check-Up

1. (Who)/ When │ opens the box?
2. │ How /(Which)│ is shorter?
3. (Who)/ Where │ starts first?
4. (Which)/ How │ comes first?
5. (What)/ Where │ does she want?

A

p. 13

1. Who makes a noise? ⭕
2. Who do you want to eat, pizza or salad? ❌
3. What makes you cry? ⭕
4. Which is yours? ⭕
5. How likes apples? ❌

B

p. 13

1. Which do you like better, this or that? — Who
2. Who can read this book?
3. What makes him so sad? — What
4. Who can solve the problem?
5. What do you want? — Which

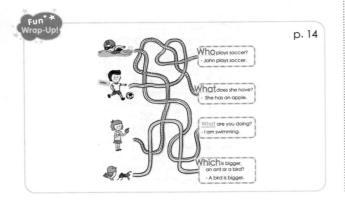

Fun Wrap-Up! p. 14

Who plays soccer?
- John plays soccer.

What does she have?
- She has an apple.

What are you doing?
- I am swimming.

Which is bigger, an ant or a bird?
- A bird is bigger.

의문형용사

p. 15

Quick Check-Up

1. │ How /(What)│ color is it?
2. (What)/ Where │ time do you go to school?
3. (Whose)/ Who │ car is this?
4. │ Who /(Whose)│ notebook is that?
5. │ Whose /(Which)│ color do you want, red or blue?

A

p. 16

1. works / Whose / mother / at school?
   Whose mother works at school?
2. Which / dress / I / should / wear?
   Which dress should I wear?
3. necklace / is / Whose / this?
   Whose necklace is this?

B

p. 16

1. Whose computer is this?
2. Whose song are you singing?
3. What time do you get up?
4. What kinds of books do you need?

Fun Wrap-Up! p. 17

What   Whose   Which

What size is this coat?
Which cup is yours?
Whose umbrella is this?
What time do you go to school?
What color do you like?

when, where, why, how

p. 18

Quick Check-Up

1. ((When)) / Where is your birthday?
2. What / ((Where)) do you go?
3. ((Why)) / How does she look so happy?
4. Where / ((How)) do you feel?
5. ((How)) / Why long is the bridge?

A

p. 19

1. ~~When~~ often do you visit your grandma?

   How often do you visit your grandma?

2. ~~What~~ do you go to school?

   How/When/Why do you go to school?

3. ~~Why~~ deep is the river?

   How deep is the river?

B

p. 19

1. _How_ do you know him?
2. _Where_ is my wallet?
3. _Why_ are you crying?
4. _How_ fast is this train?
5. _When/How_ does the movie start?

Fun Wrap-Up!

p. 20

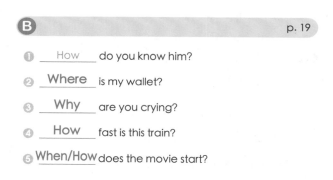
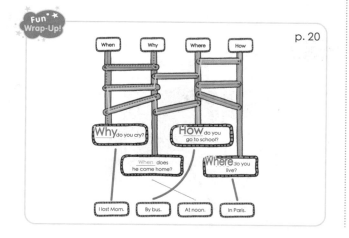

how many, how much

p. 21

Quick Check-Up

1. How many / ((How much)) water do you drink?
2. ((How many)) / How much snowmen do you make?
3. ((How many)) / How much pens does the boy have?
4. How many / ((How much)) is this ring?
5. ((How many)) / How much words does she know?

A

p. 22

1. How many students do you teach? —— O
2. How many money do you need? —— X
3. How many times did you read the book? —— O
4. How many milk does he need? —— X

B

p. 22

1. How _much_ is the car?
2. How _much_ water do you use a day?
3. How _many_ cups do we need?
4. How _many_ pairs of shoes does she have?
5. How _many_ days do I have to wait?
6. How _much_ money do you need?
7. How _many_ tables are there in the classroom?

Fun Wrap-Up!

p. 23

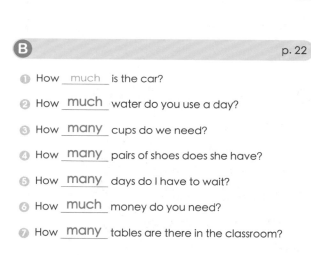

접속사 1

and, but

1. I eat pizza (and) chicken.

2. Mom (and) I eat chicken.

3. I am busy, (but) I can do it.

4. I need a pencil, an eraser, (and) three crayons.

5. I like dogs, (but) my sister doesn't like dogs.

A p. 25

1. Mike (and)/ but I need a lot of money.

2. He is handsome (and)/ but kind.

3. She likes pizza, and /(but) she doesn't like salad.

4. It's Saturday, and /(but) I don't have any plans.

5. My birthday is today, (and)/ but I have a party.

B p. 25

1. My cat is cute and sweet. — O

2. It's cold today, but I don't have a jacket. — O

3. I play the piano, and I don't play the guitar. — X

4. She likes English, and he doesn't like English. — X

5. I cut my finger, but I don't cry. — O

Answers vary.

Fun Wrap-Up! p. 26

1. I like pizza, and my brother **likes pizza** too.

2. I play soccer, but I don't play **tennis**.

3. I have a puppy, but you **don't have a puppy**

or

1. I know the answer, [but /(or)] I can't tell you.

2. Is it a boy [and /(or)] a girl?

3. You can go to the zoo by bus [but /(or)] by taxi.

4. Who opens the door, Jane [but /(or)] Tom?

A p. 28

1. I want to be a doctor ~~but~~ a nurse in the future.
   I want to be a doctor or a nurse in the future.

2. Do you have any sisters ~~but~~ brothers?
   Do you have any sisters or brothers?

3. Is your brother older ~~and~~ younger than you?
   Is your brother older or younger than you?

B p. 28

1. Do we take a train __or__ a bus?

2. Jim can't speak Japanese, __but__ he can speak English.

3. Which do you like better, apples __or__ bananas?

4. Mary goes shopping, __and__ she buys a dress.

Fun Wrap-Up! p. 29

and   but   or

1. Dad, Mom, my sister, __and__ I go to the zoo.

2. We can go there by bus __or__ by subway.

3. We pack sandwiches __and__ some fruits for lunch.

4. At the zoo, we see lions __and__ tigers.

5. I am scared, __but__ I go closer to the cage.

before, after

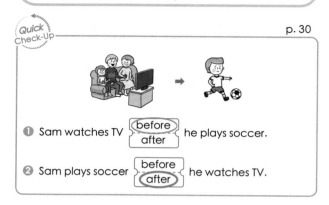

Quick Check-Up p. 30

❶ Sam watches TV __before__ / after he plays soccer.

❷ Sam plays soccer before / __after__ he watches TV.

A p. 31

❶ I raise my hand ___before___ I ask a question.

❷ I wash my face __before__ I go to school.

❸ I must go home __before__ it gets dark.

❹ I go to bed ___after___ I take a shower.

❺ I have breakfast ___after___ I get up.

B p. 31

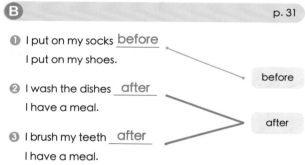

❶ I put on my socks before
I put on my shoes.

❷ I wash the dishes after
I have a meal.

❸ I brush my teeth after
I have a meal.

before

after

Fun Wrap-Up! p. 32

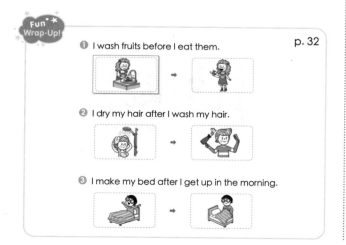

❶ I wash fruits before I eat them.

❷ I dry my hair after I wash my hair.

❸ I make my bed after I get up in the morning.

so, because

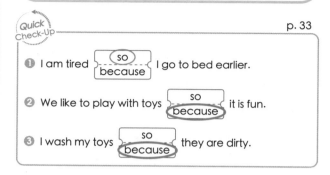

Quick Check-Up p. 33

❶ I am tired __so__ / because I go to bed earlier.

❷ We like to play with toys so / __because__ it is fun.

❸ I wash my toys so / __because__ they are dirty.

A p. 34

❶ He forgets his bag so he can't do his homework. ⭕

❷ It's cold outside because I wear a coat. ❌

❸ I buy a gift so it's her birthday. ❌

❹ I should stay in bed so I am sick. ❌

❺ I hurt my leg because I cry. ❌

B p. 34

❶ The man is hungry ___so___ he gets a snack.

❷ I study hard __because__ I have a test.

❸ He needs a fan __because__ it is summer.

❹ I get up late ___so___ I miss the school bus.

❺ Jane is sick ___so___ she can't go to school.

Fun Wrap-Up! p. 35

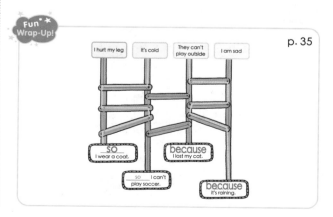

기수와 서수의 의미

Quick
Check-Up ———— p. 36

☑ one – first ☑ eleven – eleventh

☑ three – third ☐ twenty – twentyth

☐ five – fiveth ☑ sixty – sixtieth

A p. 37

first → _second_ → third → _fourth_ → fifth

→ sixth → _seventh_ → eighth → _ninth_ → tenth

B p. 37

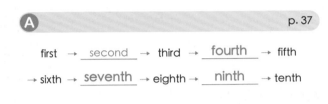

two
three
ten
nine
one
four
seven
five
eight
six

1 tenth
2 eighth
3 fifth
4 seventh
5 sixth
6 fourth
7 third
8 second
9 ninth
10 first

Fun Wrap-Up! p. 38

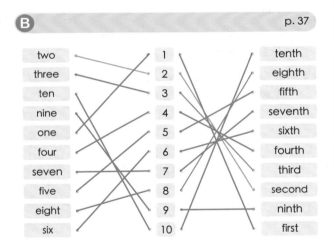

the seventh book
the second book
the fifth book
the third book
the fourth book
the sixth book
the first book

7th
6th
5th
4th
3rd
2nd
1st

연도, 날짜, 화폐, 전화번호 읽기

Quick
Check-Up ———— p. 39

☑ 1978년 – nineteen seventy eight ☐ January thirteen

☑ $100 – one hundred dollars ☑ May eleventh

A p. 40

❶ 1985년 ◯ nineteen eighty fifth ──── ✕

❷ $25 ◯ twenty five dollars ──── ◯

❸ 011-232-9990
◯ zero one one, two three two, nine nine nine oh ◯

❹ May 14 ◯ May fourteenth ──── ◯

B p. 40

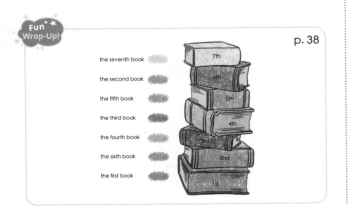

❶ July 3
July third

❷ $20
twenty dollars

❸ 2018
two thousand and eighteen
/twenty eighteen

Fun Wrap-Up! p. 41

① Tuesday June 14, 2018

Today was the wonderful day.
On my way to school, I met an old lady.
She carried a heavy bag, so I helped her.
She asked me my phone number. ②
I gave her Mom's number. 010-123-4567.

When I arrived home, Mom said, "I heard you helped an
old lady. I'm proud of you." Mom gave me $10. ③
I felt great. What a good day!

① June fourteenth, two thousand and eighteen
② zero one zero[oh one oh], one two three,
    four five six seven
③ ten dollars

Basic Test

A   p. 42

1 _____ is your birthday?
   ① What   ② Where   ③When

2 _____ color do you want, red or blue?
   ①Which   ② Whose   ③ Who

3 _____ often do you visit your grandma?
   ① When   ②How   ③ Where

4 She likes pizza, _____ she doesn't like salad.
   ① and   ② or   ③but

5 I wash my face _____ I go to school.
   ①before   ② after   ③ but

B   p. 42

1 It can be black _____or_____ grey.

2 Tomorrow is __July third__.

3 ___What___ time do you go to bed?

4 The baby falls down _____so_____ he cries.

C   p. 43

1 it? / can / you / make / How
   How can you make it?

2 at school? / mother / Whose / works
   Whose mother works at school?

3 times / the book? / did / read / How many / you
   How many times did you read the book?

4 too / can't / sleep / I / because / it's / noisy.
   I can't sleep because it's too noisy.

D *Answers vary.*   p. 43

1 What's the date today?
   It is July first.

2 How are you today?
   I'm great.

3 Which do you like better, apples or oranges?
   I like apples better.

4 What do you do before you go to bed?
   I take a shower.

명령문

p. 46

Quick Check-Up

- ☑ Pick up the book.
- ☐ Goes to the store.
- ☐ Does not run.
- ☑ Be honest.
- ☑ Do it now.
- ☐ Doesn't swim in the lake.
- ☑ Give me the pen.
- ☐ Does pass me the book.
- ☐ You quiet.
- ☑ Don't tell a lie.

A
p. 47

① ~~Takes~~ me to the store.   Take me to the store.

② ~~Writing~~ your name on the paper.
Write your name on the paper.

③ ~~Not~~ leave your bike in the park.
Don't leave your bike in the park.

④ ~~Are~~ careful.   Be careful.

⑤ ~~Does~~ not take the bus.   Do not take the bus.

B
p. 47

① (Wipe)/ Wipes the floor.

② (Don't)/ Doesn't give up.

③ (Give)/ Giving me some water.

④ Not /(Don't) be late.

⑤ (Wait)/ Waiting for me.

Fun Wrap-Up!
p. 48

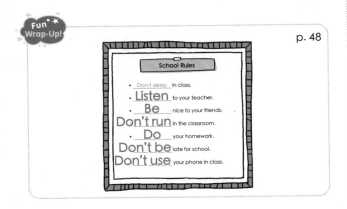

School Rules
- Don't sleep in class.
- Listen to your teacher.
- Be nice to your friends.
- Don't run in the classroom.
- Do your homework.
- Don't be late for school.
- Don't use your phone in class.

제안문

p. 49

Quick Check-Up

① Let's (dance)/ dancing .

② Let's (leave)/ be leaving him alone.

③ Let's (not wait)/ wait not for him.

④ Let's (play)/ plays soccer.

⑤ Let's (not tell)/ tell not it to Mom.

⑥ Let's (do)/ does our best.

A
p. 50

① Let's goes on a picnic. ✗

② Let's not make a noise. ○

③ Let's is honest. ✗

④ Let's play baseball. ○

B
p. 50

① play / Let's / outside.
Let's play outside.

② tomorrow. / go fishing / Let's
Let's go fishing tomorrow.

③ not / Let's / on the street. / throw trash
Let's not throw trash on the street.

④ fight / Let's / not / again.
Let's not fight again.

Fun Wrap-Up!
p. 51

① Let's not draw on the desks

② Let's not throw trash on the street.

③ Let's not be late

How 감탄문

p. 52

Quick Check-Up

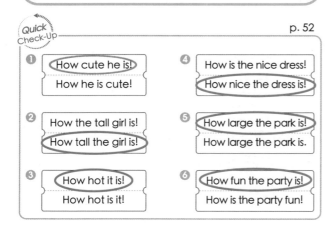

① (How cute he is!) / How he is cute!

② How the tall girl is! / (How tall the girl is!)

③ (How hot it is!) / How hot is it!

④ How is the nice dress! / (How nice the dress is!)

⑤ (How large the park is!) / How large the park is.

⑥ (How fun the party is!) / How is the party fun!

A
p. 53

① How big / are! / his feet

How big his feet are!

② your house / is! / How clean

How clean your house is!

③ How delicious / the noodle / is!

How delicious the noodle is!

④ he / How fast / eats!

How fast he eats!

B
p. 53

① How fun ~~is the game~~! → How fun the game is!

② How big her eyes are~~,~~ → How big her eyes are!

③ How lazy ~~is she~~! → How lazy she is!

④ How ~~the river deep~~ is! → How deep the river is!

⑤ How ~~you creative~~ are! → How creative you are!

Fun Wrap-Up!
p. 54

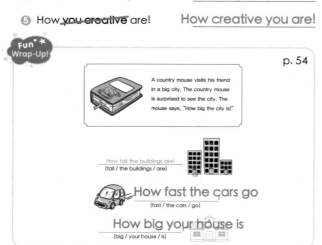

A country mouse visits his friend in a big city. The country mouse is surprised to see the city. The mouse says, "How big the city is!"

How tall the buildings are!
(tall / the buildings / are)

How fast the cars go
(fast / the cars / go)

How big your house is
(big / your house / is)

What 감탄문

p. 55

Quick Check-Up

① What a big balloon is it! ☒

② What a nice jacket! ☐O

③ What handsome man he is! ☒

④ What an old computer it is! ☐O

⑤ What nice day it is! ☒

⑥ What a funny story it is! ☐O

A
p. 56

① this / is! / What / a / beautiful picture

What a beautiful picture this is!

② an / it / is! / interesting book / What

What an interesting book it is!

③ a / little hamster / What / is! / it

What a little hamster it is!

④ What / a / great idea / it / is!

What a great idea it is!

B
p. 56

① She is a great cook.

What a great cook she is!

② It is an amazing story.

What an amazing story it is!

③ It is a cold day.

What a cold day it is!

Fun Wrap-Up!
p. 57

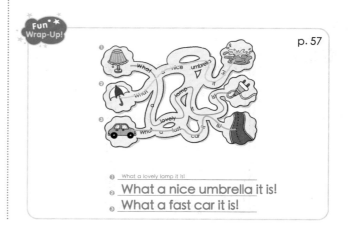

① What a lovely lamp it is!

② What a nice umbrella it is!

③ What a fast car it is!

비인칭 주어 it (1)

p. 58

Quick Check-Up

1 It is ten o'clock.

2 It is December 12.

3 It is ten meters from here to there.

4 It is Friday.

5 It is cloudy.

A
p. 59

1 It is sunny.

2 It is ten o'clock.

3 It is Friday.

4 It is March 10.

It is May 15.

It is very cold.

It is 8:30 a.m.

It is Sunday.

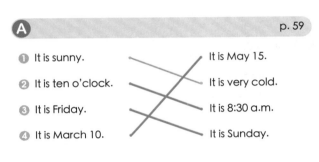

B
p. 59

4 It is March 2 today.

   Today is my first day of 4th grade.

5 It is sunny today.

3 It is 8:00 a.m. My school starts at 9:00.

2 It takes 10 minutes from home to school.

Fun Wrap-Up!
p. 60

비인칭 주어 it (2)

p. 61

Quick Check-Up

1 What time is it?

2 How far is it?

3 What day is it?

4 How's the weather?

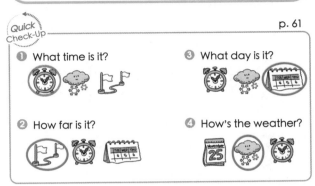

A
p. 62

1 What's the date today?

2 How's the weather?

3 How far is it?

4 What day is it?

5 What time is it?

It is Sunday.

It takes three hours.

It is July 27.

It is raining.

It is 10:30 a.m.

B
p. 62

1 A: How's the weather?
   B: It is snowy.   1

2 A: What time is it?
   B: It is 10:30 a.m.   5

3 A: What's the date today?
   B: It is November 25.   4

4 A: What day is it?
   B: It is Wednesday.   3

5 A: How far is it?
   B: It is 10 miles.   2

Fun Wrap-Up!
p. 63

A   p. 64

1 _____ careful.
  ① Are   ②Be   ③ Is

2 _____ not take the bus.
  ① Be   ② Does   ③Do

3 Let's _____ him alone.
  ① be leaving   ② leaving   ③leave

4 _____ delicious the noodle is!
  ① What   ② How often   ③How

5 _____ a great idea!
  ① How   ②What   ③ Let's

B   p. 64

1   How   fast the cars go!
2   Be   nice to your friends.
3   What   a little hamster it is!
4   It   is March 2 today.

C   p. 65

1 tell / lie. / Don't / a
  Don't tell a lie.

2 on the street. / Let's / throw / not / trash
  Let's not throw trash on the street.

3 How / you / creative / are!
  How creative you are!

4 old / What / it / is! / computer / an
  What an old computer it is!

D   *Answers vary.*   p. 65

1 How is the weather today?
  It's sunny.

2 What time is it now?
  It's 3 o'clock.

3 What day is it today?
  It's Friday.

4 How far is it from here to your school?
  It takes 10 minutes.

Be동사: 과거형

주어의 인칭에 따른 변화

p. 68

① I (was) tall and slim.
② You (were) in Paris.
③ She (was) a good teacher.
④ My pet is sick.
⑤ He is a singer.
⑥ You are so sweet.
⑦ I am kind and smart.
⑧ He (was) in the store.

A
p. 69

① He (was) / were
② We was / (were)
③ They was / (were)
④ It (was) / were
⑤ She (was) / were
⑥ I (was) / were
⑦ You was / (were)

B
p. 69

① I am in danger. ◯ I was in danger.
② He is excited. ◯ He was excited.
③ They are angry. ◯ They were angry.
④ She is ten years old. ◯ She was ten years old.
⑤ We are at the zoo. ◯ We were at the zoo.
⑥ It is cold. ◯ It was cold.

p. 70

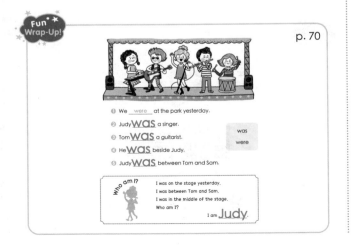

① We __were__ at the park yesterday.
② Judy was a singer.
③ Tom was a guitarist.
④ He was beside Judy.
⑤ Judy was between Tom and Sam.

was
were

Who am I?
I was on the stage yesterday.
I was between Tom and Sam.
I was in the middle of the stage.
Who am I?
I am Judy.

주어의 수에 따른 변화

p. 71

☑ This was
☐ Those was
☑ That was
☐ These was
☐ His cake were
☐ Our teachers was
☑ You and I were
☑ I was
☐ The desk were
☑ His love was

A
p. 72

① The pencils was / (were) on the table.
② That (was) / were a surprising news.
③ There was / (were) many books in her bag.
④ His brothers and sisters was / (were) in the room.
⑤ There (was) / were a flower on the ground.

B
p. 72

We __were__ angry yesterday.

There __was__ a school last month.

p. 73

was   were

I was so sad last night.
Me too! I was also happy last night.
You were happy, not me! Mom and Dad were very mean to me.
They were always so nice to you. I know.
No, I was so hungry, but there was no food on the table.
I see. You were hungry last night, but your mom and dad didn't leave any food. So you were sad.

Be동사 과거 시제: 부정문

was not, were not

p. 74

☑ He was not happy.　　☐ That not was a great movie.

☐ I not was a teacher.　　☑ There were not books.

☑ She was not cute.　　☐ He were not kind.

☐ It were not long.　　☑ They were not teachers.

A p. 75

① These fruits ___were not fresh___. (were fresh)

② The boy **was not in the room**. (was in the room)

③ The TV show **was not interesting**. (was interesting)

④ They ___were not happy___. (were happy)

⑤ He ___was not my uncle___. (was my uncle)

B p. 75

① The books / not / good stories. / were
　The books were not good stories.

② not / a good singer. / She / was
　She was not a good singer.

③ closed / The stores / not / were / yesterday.
　The stores were not closed yesterday.

④ doctors / We / not / were / last year.
　We were not doctors last year.

Fun Wrap-Up!　*Answers vary.*

p. 76

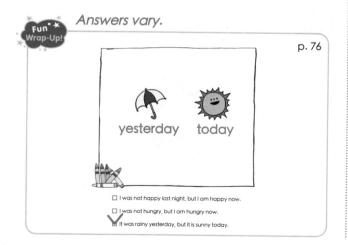

yesterday　today

☐ I was not happy last night, but I am happy now.

☐ I was not hungry, but I am hungry now.

☑ It was rainy yesterday, but it is sunny today.

wasn't, weren't

p. 77

☑ I wasn't at home.　　☐ It was't boring.

☑ There weren't pencils.　　☑ The food wasn't fresh.

☐ She wasnot tall.　　☐ He weren't kind.

☐ There weren't a book.　　☑ We weren't surprised.

A p. 78

① You weren't happy. ── ⭕

② There wasn't a book. ── ⭕

③ I wasn't in a hurry. ── ⭕

④ There weren't enough food. ── ❌

⑤ All schools weren't open. ── ⭕

B p. 78

① The juice was fresh.
　The juice wasn't fresh.

② There was Mom in the living room.
　There wasn't Mom in the living room.

③ I was taller than you.
　I wasn't taller than you.

④ There were two tables in the living room.
　There weren't two tables in the living room.

Fun Wrap-Up!

p. 79

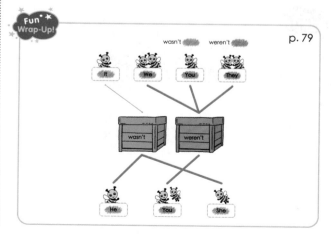

Be동사 과거 시제: 의문문

질문하기

Quick Check-Up — p. 80

1. (Was) / Were he a doctor?
2. Was / (Were) the apples on the table?
3. (Was) / Were the movie fun last night?
4. (Was) / Were your mom angry yesterday?

A
p. 81

1. We were at the museum. — Were we at the museum?
2. There were many books. — Were there many books?
3. The tickets were expensive. — Were the tickets expensive?
4. The zoo was crowded. — Was the zoo crowded?
5. It was a happy day. — Was it a happy day?

B
p. 81

1. you / 10 years old / two years ago? / Were
   Were you 10 years old two years ago?

2. Was / a good / your partner / driver?
   Was your partner a good driver?

3. on the table? / Was / there / a spoon
   Was there a spoon on the table?

Fun Wrap-Up! — p. 82

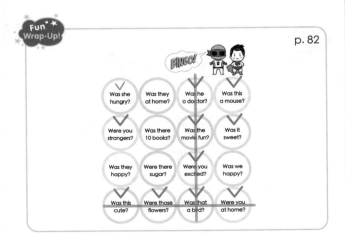

BINGO!

Was she hungry?	Was they at home?	Was he a doctor?	Was this a mouse?
Were you strangers?	Was there 10 books?	Was the movie fun?	Was it sweet?
Was they happy?	Were there sugar?	Were you excited?	Was we happy?
Was this cute?	Were those flowers?	Was that a bird?	Were you at home?

대답하기

Quick Check-Up — p. 83

1. Was he a student?
   ☑ Yes, he was.
   ☐ Yes, I was.

2. Were you a teacher?
   ☐ Yes, I were.
   ☑ No, I wasn't.

3. Were your sisters angry?
   ☐ Yes, they weren't.
   ☑ Yes, they were.

4. Was there a cat?
   ☐ Yes, there were.
   ☑ No, there wasn't.

A
p. 84

1. Was there a book? — Yes, you were.
2. Were you excited? — No, she wasn't.
3. Were we in danger? — No, it wasn't.
4. Was she happy? — No, I wasn't.
5. Was it his bag? — Yes, there was.

B
p. 84

1. Was John sad?
   Yes, he was.

2. Were they at the zoo?
   Yes, they were.

3. Was there a book on the table?
   No, there wasn't[was not].

Fun Wrap-Up! — p. 85

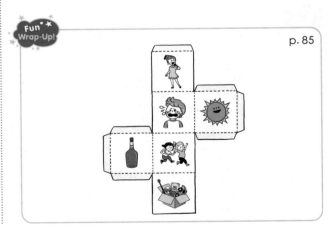

규칙 변화 (1)

p. 86

Quick Check-Up

1. I open my eyes. — **present** / past
2. I talked to Mom. — present / **past**
3. The baby speaks funny words. — **present** / past
4. They called me last night. — present / **past**
5. Mom and Dad loved me. — present / **past**

A

p. 87

1. I play / **played** soccer last night.
2. They watch / **watched** TV yesterday.
3. Babies jump / **jumped** on the bed one hour ago.
4. The lady opens / **opened** the door yesterday.
5. I clean / **cleaned** my room last night.

B

p. 87

1. I brush my teeth. → I ___brushed___ my teeth.
2. I wash my face. → I ___washed___ my face.
3. Mom talks to me. → Mom ___talked___ to me.
4. Dad loves me. → Dad ___loved___ me.
5. We laugh out loud. → We ___laughed___ out loud.

Fun Wrap-Up!

p. 88

past simple   present simple

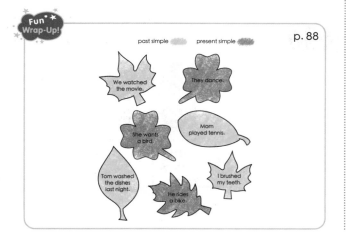

규칙 변화 (2)

p. 89

Quick Check-Up

1. I **dried** / dryed my hair one hour ago.
2. The girl **dropped** / droped her ice cream.
3. He rubed / **rubbed** his tummy.

A

p. 90

1. He finishes the book yesterday. — _finished_
2. I stay at the library last night. — stayed
3. Tom moves to a new house yesterday. — moved
4. Max stops his car. — stopped
5. The baby cries 10 minutes ago. — cried
6. I love my family. — loved

B

p. 90

1. He ~~planed~~ his summer vacation. — _planned_
2. She ~~tryed~~ to open the heavy door. — tried
3. They ~~danceed~~ happily. — danced
4. She ~~enjoied~~ the movie. — enjoyed
5. We ~~liveed~~ in that house one year ago. — lived

Fun Wrap-Up!

p. 91

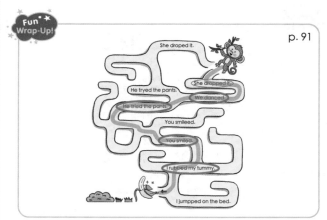

일반동사: 과거 시제 2

불규칙 변화 (1)

Quick Check-Up p. 92

1 I (put)/ putted the book in my bag.

2 It (cost)/ costed a lot.

3 You (hurt)/ hurted my leg.

4 He (cut)/ cutted his finger.

5 We (read)/ readed a book last night.

6 I (set)/ setted my watch yesterday.

A p. 93

1 She hurt her leg two days ago. present /(past)

2 She puts down the cake. (present)/ past

3 Mom read a book last night. present /(past)

4 I set the table for Mom yesterday. present /(past)

5 The ticket cost $15 last night. present /(past)

B p. 93

1 The meal ___cost___ me $10 last month.

2 He ___set___ his watch yesterday.

3 I ___hurt___ my knee yesterday.

4 My friend ___read___ the book last week.

5 She ___hit___ the ball.

Fun Wrap-Up! p. 94

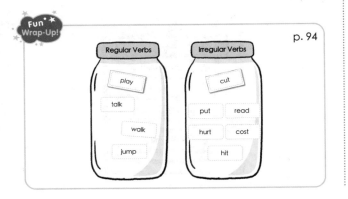

불규칙 변화 (2)

Quick Check-Up p. 95

1 swimed / (swam)

2 (drank) / drinked

3 singed / (sang)

4 runed / (ran)

A p. 96

1 Dave ___ate___ a slice of pizza. (eat)

2 They ___sat___ on the bench. (sit)

3 He ___told___ a fairy tale to his children. (tell)

4 The man ___made___ a robot. (make)

5 They ___went___ to the zoo. (go)

B p. 96

1 I drawed /(drew) pictures last night.

2 Mom buyed /(bought) some books.

3 The boy sleeped /(slept) on the bed.

4 She gived /(gave) me a gift.

5 I heared /(heard) a noise.

6 The cats runned /(ran) fast.

Fun Wrap-Up! p. 97

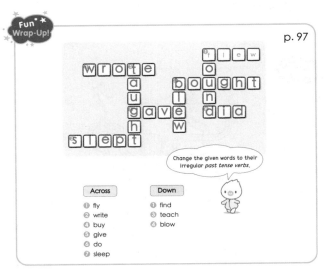

Change the given words to their irregular *past tense verbs*.

Across	Down
1 fly	1 find
2 write	3 teach
4 buy	4 blow
5 give	
6 do	
7 sleep	

일반동사 과거 시제: 부정문

did not

p. 98

Quick Check-Up

❶ The boy ___∨___ tell me _____ the story.

❷ I ___∨___ have _____ time.

❸ We ___∨___ play _____ in the park.

❹ They ___∨___ hit _____ the ball.

❺ He ___∨___ give _____ me a book.

A
p. 99

❶ They _____did not eat_____ lunch at the cafe. (ate)

❷ I __did not watch__ TV yesterday. (watched)

❸ She ___did not open___ the door. (opened)

❹ Susan ___did not like___ the movie. (liked)

❺ Mom ___did not give___ me money. (gave)

B
p. 99

❶ did not / put on / Jane / a shirt.
   Jane did not put on a shirt.

❷ They / cut / did not / the ribbon.
   They did not cut the ribbon.

❸ You / paint / did not / the wall.
   You did not paint the wall.

Fun Wrap-Up!

p. 100

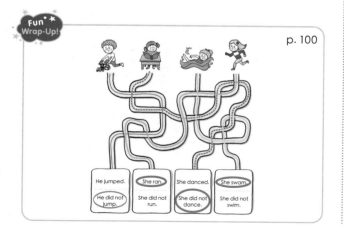

didn't

p. 101

Quick Check-Up

❶ She ___∨___ study _____ English.

❷ Sam ___∨___ read _____ the books.

❸ I ___∨___ play _____ the piano yesterday.

❹ Dad ___∨___ drive _____ a car.

❺ We ___∨___ watch _____ the movie.

❻ The students ___∨___ sing _____ a song for us.

A
p. 102

❶ I didn't ~~forgot~~ my book.   forget

❷ The singers didn't ~~arrived~~ late.   arrive

❸ She didn't ~~traveled~~ to London.   travel

❹ He didn't ~~danced~~ yesterday.   dance

❺ We didn't ~~watched~~ the film.   watch

B
p. 102

❶ She ___didn't answer___ the phone. (answered)

❷ She ___didn't enjoy___ the festival. (enjoyed)

❸ I ___didn't play___ with my friends. (played)

❹ I ___didn't wash___ the vases. (washed)

❺ They ___didn't clean___ my room. (cleaned)

Fun Wrap-Up!

p. 103

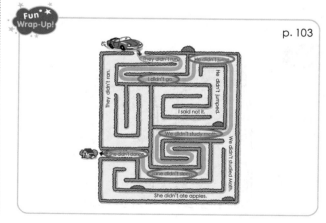

일반동사 과거 시제: 의문문

Did ~?

p. 104

☑ Did the roses smell good?

☑ Did you listen to music?

☑ Did he hurt himself?

☐ Did they cleaned the room?

☐ Did you liked your puppy?

A

p. 105

1 Tim set the table last night. (set - set)
   ➡ Did Tim set the table last night?

2 The young lady slept on the bed. (sleep - slept)
   ➡ Did the young lady sleep on the bed?

3 Hanna drove the car to the store. (drive - drove)
   ➡ Did Hanna drive the car to the store?

B

p. 105

1 Did you finished / (finish) the book?

2 Did you played / (play) soccer?

3 Did you hear the story?
   - Yes, I (did) / do .

4 Did they know each other?
   - No, they (didn't) / weren't .

p. 106

| Yes, they did. | Yes, he did. | Yes, she did. |
| No, they didn't. | No, he didn't. | No, she didn't. |

1 Did the family go to the zoo?   Yes, they did.
2 Did they see tigers at the zoo?   Yes, they did.
3 Did the man carry a bag?   No, he didn't.
4 Did the boy wear a cap?   Yes, he did.
5 Did the girl wear glasses?   No, she didn't.

의문사+did ~?

p. 107

1 Where (did) / do you go yesterday?

2 What (did) / were you do last night?

3 When (did) / was he call me?

4 Why (did) / do the baby cry last night?

5 Who (did) / were you see?

A

p. 108

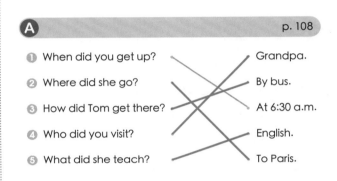

1 When did you get up?   Grandpa.
2 Where did she go?   By bus.
3 How did Tom get there?   At 6:30 a.m.
4 Who did you visit?   English.
5 What did she teach?   To Paris.

B

p. 108

1 did / When / she / meet / her friends?
   When did she meet her friends?

2 you / did / cry / Why / last night?
   Why did you cry last night?

3 did / go / Where / they / after school?
   Where did they go after school?

p. 109

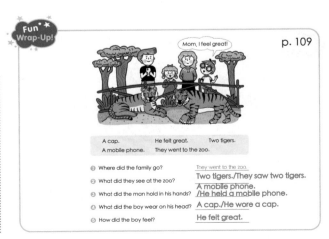

Mom, I feel great!

| A cap. | He felt great. | Two tigers. |
| A mobile phone. | They went to the zoo. | |

1 Where did the family go?   They went to the zoo.
2 What did they see at the zoo?   Two tigers./They saw two tigers.
3 What did the man hold in his hands? A mobile phone. /He held a mobile phone.
4 What did the boy wear on his head? A cap./He wore a cap.
5 How did the boy feel?   He felt great.

긍정문

p. 110

Quick Check-Up

- ☑ Steve and Sally were singing.
- ☐ We was eating some ice cream.
- ☐ I were reading a book.
- ☑ You were listening to music.
- ☐ She is talking on the phone yesterday.

A
p. 111

1. She (was)/ were reading a book.
2. The bees was /(were) buzzing.
3. He (was)/ were playing soccer.
4. We was /(were) dancing.
5. Tom and Marry was /(were) walking on the street.

B
p. 111

1. They ___were swimming___ . (swim)
2. He ___was sleeping___ on the couch. (sleep)
3. We ___were having___ breakfast. (have)
4. Sara ___was painting___ the fence. (paint)
5. I ___was washing___ my hands. (wash)

Fun Wrap-Up!

p. 112

When you visited us . . .
1. Dad ___was cooking___ lunch. (cook)
2. Mom ___was reading___ a book. (read)
3. Grandpa ___was taking___ a nap on the couch. (take)
4. Grandma ___was drinking___ a cup of coffee. (drink)

부정문

p. 113

Quick Check-Up

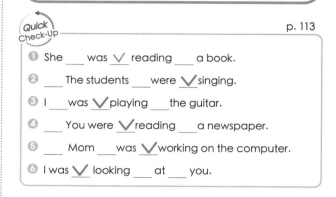

1. She ___ was ✓ reading ___ a book.
2. ___ The students ___ were ✓ singing.
3. I ___ was ✓ playing ___ the guitar.
4. ___ You were ✓ reading ___ a newspaper.
5. ___ Mom ___ was ✓ working on the computer.
6. I was ✓ looking ___ at ___ you.

A
p. 114

1. I ___wasn't___ dancing. I was reading books.
2. Jim ___wasn't___ singing songs in the concert. He was playing the violin.
3. I ___was___ knocking on the door, but you didn't hear it.

B
p. 114

1. Jack was not answering the phone. He ___was drying___ his hair. (dry)
2. Tom wasn't watching TV. He __was reading__ a book. (read)
3. Jane wasn't eating a banana. She ___was eating___ an apple. (eat)

Fun Wrap-Up!

p. 115

Lesson 58 과거 진행형: 의문문

yes/no 의문문

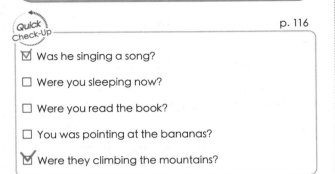

Quick Check-Up — p. 116

- ☑ Was he singing a song?
- ☐ Were you sleeping now?
- ☐ Were you read the book?
- ☐ You was pointing at the bananas?
- ☑ Were they climbing the mountains?

A — p. 117

① She was looking at the flowers.
→ Was she looking at the flowers?

② Tom was having breakfast.
→ Was Tom having breakfast?

③ He was thinking about the plan.
→ Was he thinking about the plan?

④ They were looking into the mirror.
→ Were they looking into the mirror?

B — p. 117

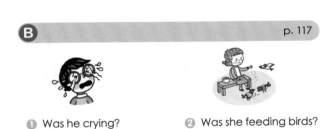

① Was he crying?
- Yes, he was.

② Was she feeding birds?
- Yes, she was.

Fun Wrap-Up! — p. 118

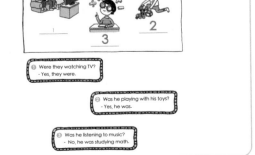

① Were they watching TV?
- Yes, they were.

② Was he playing with his toys?
- Yes, he was.

③ Was he listening to music?
- No, he was studying math.

의문사 있는 의문문

Quick Check-Up — p. 119

① Where were you going?
- ☑ To the hospital.
- ☐ Yes, I was.

② Who was running?
- ☑ Jane.
- ☐ To the market.

③ What were they doing?
- ☑ Homework.
- ☐ No, they weren't.

④ Why was she crying?
- ☑ She cut her fingers.
- ☐ Yes, she was.

A — p. 120

① were / Why / reading / you / books?
Why were you reading books?

② When / they / listening to music? / were
When were they listening to music?

③ Where / she / was / going?
Where was she going?

④ he / eating? / What / was
What was he eating?

B — p. 120

① What were you doing?
- I was running. — ⭕

② Who were you talking to?
- Yes, I was. — ❌

③ When were they listening to music?
- At 7:00 p.m. — ⭕

Fun Wrap-Up! — p. 121

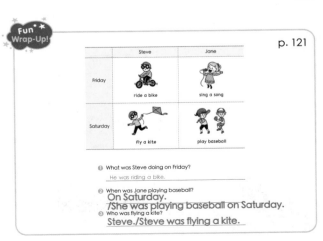

	Steve	Jane
Friday	ride a bike	sing a song
Saturday	fly a kite	play baseball

① What was Steve doing on Friday?
He was riding a bike.

② When was Jane playing baseball?
On Saturday.
/She was playing baseball on Saturday.

③ Who was flying a kite?
Steve./Steve was flying a kite.

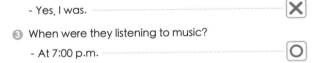

A   p. 122

1 Babies _____ on the bed one hour ago.
   ① jump   ② jumps   ③ jumped

2 I _____ a noise.
   ① heared   ② heard   ③ hears

3 Susan _____ the movie.
   ① didn't like   ② didn't liked   ③ doesn't liked

4 Where were you going? - _____
   ① Yes, I was.   ② No, I wasn't. ③ To the hospital.

5 When did you get up? - _____
   ① By bus.   ② At 6:30 a.m.   ③ To Paris.

B   p. 122

1 He _____told_____ a fairy tale to his children.
2 Who _____was_____ running?
3 _____Was_____ the movie fun last night?
4 They _____were_____ talking about football.

C   p. 123

1 Were / expensive? / the tickets
   Were the tickets expensive?

2 He / was / me / taller than / last year.
   He was taller than me last year.

3 yesterday. / closed / were / not / The stores
   The stores were not closed yesterday.

4 Were / looking / they / into the mirror?
   Were they looking into the mirror?

D *Answers vary.*   p. 123

1 How old were you last year?
   I was 9 years old.

2 What did you do yesterday?
   I watched TV.

3 What did you eat for breakfast today?
   I ate an apple.

4 Did you cut your nails yesterday?
   Yes, I did.

Lesson 59 미래 시제

will

p. 126

Quick Check-Up

❶ He ∨ be ___ a soccer player ___.

❷ ___ She ∨ play ___ tennis tomorrow.

❸ I ∨ not ___ drive my car to ___ the school.

A p. 127

❶ I ___will finish___ the book by 5 p.m. (finish)

❷ I ___will be___ a firefighter in the future. (be)

❸ They ___will work___ in the garden tomorrow. (work)

❹ I ___will open___ the window. (open)

❺ It ___will rain___ this weekend. (rain)

B p. 127

❶ I ~~buy~~ a new pen tomorrow. ___will buy___

❷ She ~~is~~ ten years old next year. ___will be___

❸ I ~~go~~ to the beach soon. ___will go___

❹ I ~~get up~~ early tomorrow morning. ___will get up___

❺ He ~~watches~~ the movie next Sunday. ___will watch___

❻ They ~~played~~ basketball next weekend. ___will play___

Fun Wrap-Up! p. 128

❶ I ___will have breakfast___ at 10:00 a.m. (have breakfast)

❷ I ___will play baseball___ at 2:00 p.m. (play baseball)

❸ I ___will read a book___ at 5:00 p.m. (read a book)

❹ I ___will watch TV___ at 8:00 p.m. (watch TV)

be going to

p. 129

Quick Check-Up

◿ tomorrow ◿ next month ◳ yesterday

◿ in three years ◳ last night ◿ two years later

◿ soon ◳ last Sunday ◳ three hours ago

◿ next week ◿ in the future ◿ next Saturday

A p. 130

❶ We ___are going to clean___ the room. (clean)

❷ We ___are going to watch___ TV tomorrow evening. (watch)

❸ They ___are going to go fishing___ next week. (go fishing)

❹ I ___am going to read___ a storybook later. (read)

❺ I ___am going to climb___ the mountain tomorrow. (climb)

B p. 130

❶ is going to / My son / play basketball / tomorrow.
___My son is going to play basketball tomorrow.___

❷ visit / He / this summer. / is going to / his cousin
___He is going to visit his cousin this summer.___

❸ I'm / study / going to / English / this weekend.
___I'm going to study English this weekend.___

Fun Wrap-Up! p. 131

❶ Amy ___is going to visit___ her grandma. (visit)

❷ Tom ___is going to play___ soccer. (play)

❸ Jack ___is going to read___ a book. (read)

❹ Janet ___is going to swim___ . (swim)

❺ Hera ___is going to climb___ the mountains with her friend. (climb)

미래 시제: 의문문

will 의문문

p. 132

Quick Check-Up

❶ Will you (go / going) to the store?

❷ Will they (eating / eat) pizza for lunch?

❸ What will you (do / did) after school?

❹ Will David (invites / invite) us to his party?

❺ Will Tom and Jane (sing / singing) a song?

❻ What time will he (visits / visit) us?

A p. 133

❶ you / Will / go fishing?   Will you go fishing?

❷ buy the pen? / she / Will   Will she buy the pen?

❸ they / Will / take a taxi?   Will they take a taxi?

❹ do / on Sunday? / will / What / you
  What will you do on Sunday?

❺ will / you / When / go shopping?
  When will you go shopping?

B p. 133

❶ What will Tom and Suzy do tomorrow?
  - They (will have / have) a party.

❷ When will he meet her?
  - He (meets / will meet) her next month.

❸ Will they play baseball tomorrow?
  - No, (they will / they won't).

Fun Wrap-Up! p. 134

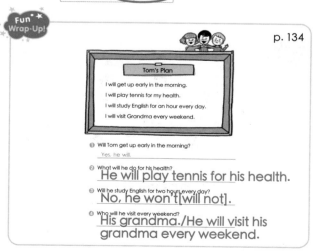

Tom's Plan

I will get up early in the morning.
I will play tennis for my health.
I will study English for an hour every day.
I will visit Grandma every weekend.

❶ Will Tom get up early in the morning?
  Yes, he will.

❷ What will he do for his health?
  He will play tennis for his health.

❸ Will he study English for two hours every day?
  No, he won't[will not].

❹ Who will he visit every weekend?
  His grandma./He will visit his grandma every weekend.

be going to 의문문

p. 135

Quick Check-Up

❶ (Are / Will) you going to ride this bike?

❷ (Is / Are) you going to stay at home?

❸ (Are / Is) he going to paint the walls?

❹ (Will / Is) John going to fix his toy car?

❺ (Is / Are) they going to go fishing?

A p. 136

❶ you / going to / study English / Are / tomorrow?
  Are you going to study English tomorrow?

❷ are / you / going to / What time / get up?
  What time are you going to get up?

❸ are / you / When / going to / go to bed / tonight?
  When are you going to go to bed tonight?

❹ going to / are / you / What /eat for lunch?
  What are you going to eat for lunch?

B p. 136

❶ Are you going to have lunch now?
  - No, I (am not / am). I am going to have a rest.

❷ Is he going to buy a new toy?
  - Yes, he (isn't / is). He's going to (buys / buy) one.

❸ Are they going to wash the car tomorrow?
  - (Yes / No), they aren't. They're going to (fix / fixes) it.

Fun Wrap-Up! p. 137

Is he going to study?

Are you going to swim?

What are you going to do?

What is she going to do?

Yes, I am.

I'm going to play soccer.

No, he isn't.

She is going to read a book.

Basic Test

A
p. 138

1 I _____ read a storybook later.
   ① are going to ②am going to ③ is going to

2 We _____ clean the room.
   ① is going to ②are going to ③ am going to

3 He will meet her _____.
   ①next month ② yesterday ③ last weekend

4 What will Tom and Suzy do _____?
   ① last month ②tomorrow ③ two hours ago

5 Will they play baseball tomorrow? - No, _____.
   ① they were ② they will ③they won't

B
p. 138

1 She is not going to come home _this weekend_

2 I _will open_ the window.

3 Are they going to _wash_ the car tomorrow?

4 When _are you_ going to go to bed tonight?

C
p. 139

1 will / rain / It / this weekend.
   It will rain this weekend.

2 Amy / visit / is going to / her grandma.
   Amy is going to visit her grandma.

3 When / you / go fishing? / will
   When will you go fishing?

4 are / you / do / What / going to / tomorrow?
   What are you going to do tomorrow?

D *Answers vary.*
p. 139

1 What are you going to do today?
   I am going to visit my grandma.

2 What are you going to do tomorrow?
   I am going to meet my friend.

3 When will you get up tomorrow?
   I'll get up at 7 a.m.

4 What are you going to do this weekend?
   I am going to study English.

MEMO

Activity Cards & Paper Cube

Lesson 45   p. 32

Lesson 54   p. 94

put	read	play	cut	hurt
cost	talk	hit	walk	jump

Activity Cards & Paper Cube

Lesson 52 p. 85

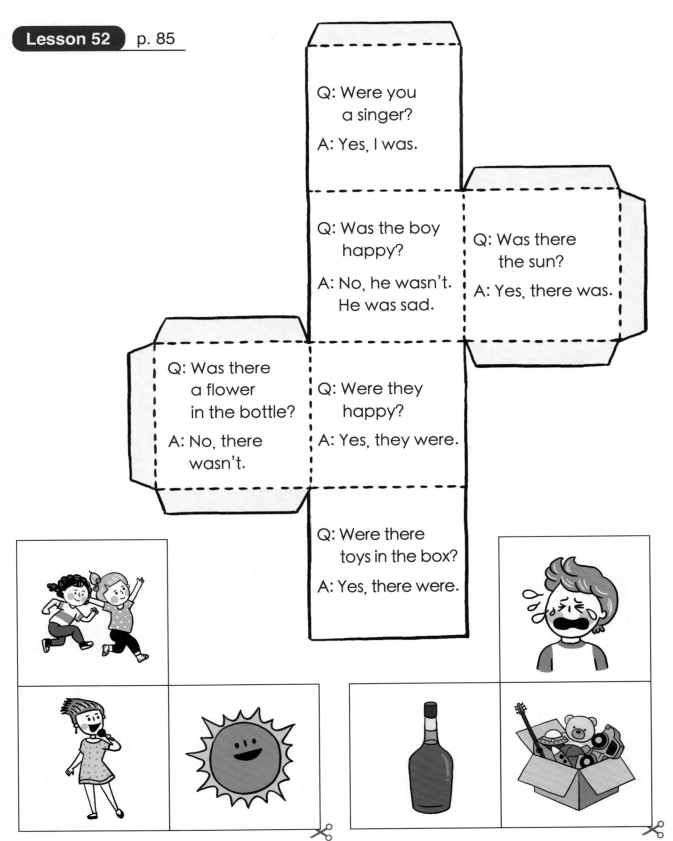

Q: Were you a singer?

A: Yes, I was.

Q: Was the boy happy?

A: No, he wasn't. He was sad.

Q: Was there the sun?

A: Yes, there was.

Q: Was there a flower in the bottle?

A: No, there wasn't.

Q: Were they happy?

A: Yes, they were.

Q: Were there toys in the box?

A: Yes, there were.

부록

Appendix

 동사 변화표

동사원형		과거형	동사원형+ing
be	~이다, 있다	was/were	being
break	깨뜨리다	broke	breaking
become	~이 되다	became	becoming
begin	시작하다	began	beginning
bend	구부리다	bent	bending
blow	불다	blew	blowing
bring	데려오다	brought	bringing
build	짓다, 세우다	built	building
buy	사다	bought	buying
catch	잡다	caught	catching
come	오다	came	coming
cost	비용이 들다	cost	costing
cut	자르다	cut	cutting
dig	파다	dug	digging
do	하다	did	doing
draw	그리다	drew	drawing
drink	마시다	drank	drinking
drive	운전하다	drove	driving
eat	먹다	ate	eating
fall	떨어지다	fell	falling

동사원형		과거형	동사원형+ing
feel	느끼다	felt	feeling
find	찾다	found	finding
fly	날다	flew	flying
forget	잊다	forgot	forgetting
get	얻다, 받다	got	getting
give	주다	gave	giving
go	가다	went	going
have	가지다, 먹다	had	having
hear	듣다	heard	hearing
hit	치다	hit	hitting
hurt	다치게 하다, 아프다	hurt	hurting
keep	지키다	kept	keeping
know	알다	knew	knowing
lay	놓다, (알을) 낳다	laid	laying
leave	떠나다	left	leaving
lie	눕다, 놓여 있다	lay	lying
lose	잃다, 지다	lost	losing
make	만들다	made	making
meet	만나다	met	meeting
pay	지불하다	paid	paying

동사원형		과거형	동사원형+ing
put	두다, 놓다	put	putting
read	읽다	read [red]	reading
ride	(탈것을) 타다	rode	riding
rise	뜨다, 떠오르다	rose	rising
run	달리다	ran	running
say	말하다	said	saying
see	보다	saw	seeing
sell	팔다	sold	selling
sing	노래하다	sang	singing
sit	앉다	sat	sitting
sleep	자다	slept	sleeping
speak	이야기하다	spoke	speaking
stand	서다	stood	standing
swim	수영하다	swam	swimming
teach	가르치다	taught	teaching
tell	말하다	told	telling
think	생각하다	thought	thinking
wear	입고 있다	wore	wearing
win	이기다	won	winning
write	쓰다	wrote	writing

My Grammar Note

✿ 빈칸에 알맞은 과거형과 동사원형+ing 형태를 써 넣으세요.

	동사원형	과거형	동사원형+ing
1	lie		
2	give		
3	think		
4	sit		
5	go		
6	buy		
7	build		
8	become		
9	catch		
10	eat		
11	leave		
12	read		
13	have		
14	hit		
15	drive		
16	begin		
17	be		
18	cut		
19	feel		
20	sing		

Answers

p. 175

	동사원형	과거형	동사원형+ing
1	lie	lay	lying
2	give	gave	giving
3	think	thought	thinking
4	sit	sat	sitting
5	go	went	going
6	buy	bought	buying
7	build	built	building
8	become	became	becoming
9	catch	caught	catching
10	eat	ate	eating
11	leave	left	leaving
12	read	read	reading
13	have	had	having
14	hit	hit	hitting
15	drive	drove	driving
16	begin	began	beginning
17	be	was/were	being
18	cut	cut	cutting
19	feel	felt	feeling
20	sing	sang	singing